# Invitation to
# Archaeology

## *2nd Edition*

## Philip Rahtz

BLACKWELL
Oxford UK & Cambridge USA

First published 1985
Reprinted 1986
Second edition published 1991

Blackwell Publishers
108 Cowley Road, Oxford, OX4 1JE, UK

3 Cambridge Center
Cambridge, Massachusetts 02142, USA

*Library of Congress Cataloging in Publication Data*
Rahtz, Philip A.
Invitation to archaeology / Philip Rahtz. – 2nd ed.
p.    cm
Originally published: 1986.
Includes bibliographical references and index.
ISBN 0–631–18067–2
1. Archaeology.   2. Archaeology–Great Britain.   I. Title.
CC165.R34   1991
930.1–dc20
91-23019
CIP

*British Library Cataloguing in Publication Data*
A CIP catalogue record for this book is available from the British Library.

Typeset in 11 on 13pt Bembo
by Graphicraft Typesetters Ltd., Hong Kong.
Printed in Great Britain
by Billing and Sons Ltd, Worcester

# Contents

To Genny, Nicky, Diana, David and Sebastian

# Preface

This book was written towards the end of a professional career in archaeology; I have passed the three score years and ten barrier, and am now on extra time, but I am still active in the field and at my desk. I began work in archaeology as an amateur and did not get paid for doing it until I was over 30.

At this stage in my career, I can afford to be honest, uninhibited and indiscreet. I can be nostalgic, garrulous, anecdotal, prejudiced and inaccurate (to quote my colleagues). It is impossible to survey the field of archaeology without setting it against one's own experience and to that extent there is inevitably a good deal of autobiography in the pages that follow.

The book is not intended as a textbook: its intention is to show that archaeology is important to people and to society, that it is immensely stimulating and educational to the individual and will enrich the life of anybody who becomes involved in it.

The audience I am writing for is anyone who feels mildly interested in or curious about archaeology, and wants to know more; the school-leaver wondering whether to study the subject at university level; the adult thinking of joining an evening class or an excavation; those with enforced (or voluntary) leisure, looking for some rewarding way of using their time; those already subscribing to popular archaeological magazines; those on treasure-hunting, ley-line, or metal-detecting expeditions – see chapter 7; anyone wanting to know more about archaeology, but unwilling to read a serious textbook; and my academic colleagues in search of light relief.

I am indebted to a very large number of people I have known in the course of my digging and academic career; I have absorbed their ideas, theories and attitudes, often with some distortion and without acknowledgement. I do, however, owe a great debt to individuals who have been especially stimulating and influential, notably Ian Burrow, Sue Hirst, Ann Woodward, Peter Leach, Priscilla Roxburgh, Mick Aston, Grenville Astill, Martin Carver (who succeeded me as professor at York) and my wife, Lorna Watts.

This is not the first book with this title. In 1967 James Deetz wrote his classic textbook, which has been used by students all over the world. I hope he will find this a worthy namesake.

# Note to Second Edition

The first edition of this book was received with considerable enthusiasm, but there was a certain amount of criticism. The latter was principally that while the book would be much appreciated by archaeologists, particularly English ones, it was less accessible to the more general reader, unacquainted with the social and intellectual scene within which archaeology is practised. This was especially directed at my attempts to be humorous, which were 'in-jokes' and would be meaningless to many people. If this is true of my English readers, I do wonder what those in other countries might feel; notably those who acquired the edition published in Portuguese (in 1985). They must have been puzzled by many of the jokes, such as the famous one concerning the Oxford archaeologist and the Yorkshire farmer (page 107), which depends on both a play of words and also some understanding of the philosophical basis of archaeological interpretation. To me, it seemed even funnier in Portuguese, but only because I didn't understand that language.

In this second edition, I have revised many parts of the book, both in the light of critical review and to take into account the changes that have affected archaeology since the book was written in the early 1980s. This applies particularly to the organizational structure of archaeology and its funding, to the expansion of interests into the European and world community, and the changes in theoretical and interpretative approaches. There is also some new material based on recent experiences, and on the involvement of the individual in the rapidly expanding scene of archaeology. Finally, there are some deletions of material that has become dated or distasteful, and new versions of two of the illustrations.

# 1

# What is Archaeology?

## DEFINITIONS

Archaeology is the study of *things*, tangible objects which can be seen and measured; what is broadly defined as material culture. This is the physical manifestation of human activities – rubbish, treasure, buildings and graves.

All of this can be examined to see what light it can shed on human behaviour. It cannot, however, be studied in isolation; we must also understand the environment in which human beings have evolved and lived. This may include factors over which they have little or no control, such as sunspots, climate and tides; it may also include the ways in which humans, among other animals (but to a vastly greater extent than, for example, beavers), have transformed the landscape, the animal world and recently the atmosphere; and the chemistry of sea, lake and river.

Archaeologists thus study not only pots and jewellery, temples and bones, ditches and mounds, but also lake sediments, beetles, animal tombs, excrement and parasites. They are normally interested in past societies, but it is important to note that this definition does not exclude the study of today's material culture. Some archaeologists study the contents of dustbins, notably in Tucson, Arizona (the 'garbage project'; Rathje, 1978). It's true that archaeology is mostly about the past, as its name implies; but when this is the case, the archaeologist is really being a historian (using this word to mean anyone who is interested in the past, rather than someone who studies documents). To make

1

any sense of past material remains, however, archaeology has to have *theory* concerning what can or cannot be deduced from material residues (that is, 'rubbish'). This can be developed by a study of modern material culture as well as that surviving from past societies (chapter 6).

We can live in an African village or in a modern city and formulate and test theory: do the contents of the dustbins of Tucson really reflect the ethnic and class divisions of the city? Can we reconstruct the university vice-chancellor's lifestyle from his dustbin and compare it with that of the self-catering student? The short answer is yes, there is a demonstrable relationship: the vice-chancellor drinks more expensive wine and eats more meat than the student; this is indicated by the bottles and bones in his dustbin.

With such improved theoretical understanding, and with the arsenal of techniques that archaeology can now deploy, we can attempt to reconstruct past human behaviour. This has in the past tended to be mainly descriptive. We have been successful in showing how people buried their dead, what their churches and temples were like, how they farmed the land and what food they ate. This is all very well, and of intrinsic interest, but nowadays archaeology is more ambitious: it seeks to deduce not only *what* happened, but *why* it happened. Why, at some times and in some places, did people cremate their dead, rather than bury them? Why has cremation gained ground (*sic*) so rapidly in the twentieth century? Why did towns develop? Did past populations increase or decrease because of climatic changes, or improved technology, or a changing economy, or combinations of several causes?

## WHY ARCHAEOLOGY?

Why should anyone want to know about the past? Most people are interested in the present, so why should a small minority be so concerned about origins and change? Answers to these weighty questions are difficult, but the reader will, it is hoped, have a better understanding after reading this book. The question, 'Why do people do archaeology?' is explored in chapter 2. Here, we may anticipate the discussion by concluding that there are two principal reasons: it is done for enjoyment, and/or because it is actually important.

I should straightaway declare my firm belief that not only is archaeology fun, highly educational and intellectually satisfying to the individual, it is also crucial to human survival on this planet, and should be accorded high priority and resources by modern society. Understanding of humankind's past is an important aid to understanding people today. It is the one subject (though others make similar claims) which is central to all knowledge. It is archaeology which uniquely can provide the total perspective of human beings on this planet. We need this to be able to take a cool, balanced look at our own society.

How can archaeology claim such a centrality among the humanities? Principally (and here also lies its immense educational value) it is precisely because of its links with other disciplines. Archaeology is not a science like biology or chemistry, though it uses scientific methods and adopts scientific attitudes. It has been described as a cultural science and has in recent years been moving closer to the social sciences than to the natural ones, for reasons that I hope will become apparent. Modern archaeology finds increasingly common ground with anthropology, philosophy, sociology and politics. It is really aiming at the same thing – the understanding of humans – by utilizing the special method of the interpretation of material residues. The obvious limitations of such an appraoch are that it is difficult to find out from material remains such as ruins and cesspit residues what people think or thought, a factor regarded as central to the other social sciences.

Archaeology's great advantage, however, is that unlike these disciplines, it can bring an enriched and broader time dimension to the study of humankind. The observation of the minds of living humans (as in the social sciences) can to some extent be extended by written sources, which are the special province of historians. These are, however, available for only the most recent past – a few thousand years at most, and in some parts of the world no more than a few generations. The archaeologist is concerned with a time-scale thousands of times longer – up to

3

five million years in Africa and the Far East, and tens of thousands in even the most recently settled areas, such as Australia or America; in remote and relatively inaccessible places alone, such as New Zealand, is the time-span of human activity to be measured only in the hundreds of years normally available to the students of written sources. Archaeology's interests cover the entire world, from Samoa to Spain, from Australia to North America; and in material from fossil human bones and stone tools to today's dustbins.

ARCHAEOLOGY AND OTHER SUBJECTS

The origins of the world and of life must be understood, in our study both of the environment and of the complex biological evolution which filled the planet with its diverse life-forms, including humans and other animals. The structure of such knowledge is illustrated in figure 1.

Human beings evolved as part of the environment, and are studied within its development. They have also been influential in altering it, and not always to our benefit, as we are now belatedly realizing. Such changes result from the profound effects of human activities on the environment (by pollution, by desiccation and also by the direct exploitation of natural resources). Large areas of the present world landscape owe their appearance to the patterns imposed by farming, industry, towns and communications (Shackley, 1981).

The most important subject with which archaeology is linked (and which it is part of) is anthropology. *Physical* anthropology deals both with the biology of living humans (for example, the study of racial types etc.) and also with the remains of past human beings, made available by archaeology. *Social* anthropology, on the other hand, is concerned primarily not with archaeology, but with recent humans as studied through the social sciences, theology, language, history and other allied disciplines. Because of the material available for their study, it is only rarely that social (or 'cultural') anthropologists are interested in origins, development and change (that is, the past).

4

# ENVIRONMENT and SOCIETY

COSMOS *(cosmology)*
|
SOLAR SYSTEM *(astronomy)*
|
EARTH *(earth sciences)*
|
ROCKS *(geology)*
|
LIFE *(biology)*

<u>extinct</u>
fossil plants and animals
*(geology, palaeontology)*

<u>surviving</u>
primates          others
| *(zoology)*
hominids *(human biology)*
|

CHANGING ENVIRONMENTAL RESOURCES AND CONSTRAINTS
anthropogenic modification
|

*HUMANS IN THE ENVIRONMENT*
*relationships with other life forms*
|
SYSTEMS IN HUMAN SOCIETY
*subsistence, technology, economy, social structure, religion*

|

STUDIED BY :

| ANTHROPOLOGY | ARCHAEOLOGY | HUMANITIES |
|---|---|---|
| *physical,* | *natural sciences,* | *philosophy* |
| *social/cultural* | *social sciences,* | *theology* |
|  | *etc.* | *history* |
| *ethnology* | *ethno-archaeology* | *linguistics* |
| *ethnography* |  | *etc.* |

*folklore*
*place names*
*'oral history'*

# *TOTAL HISTORY*

*Figure 1*   The structure of knowledge of the
environment and society

All these disciplines contribute to the understanding of humans in the environment; only interdisciplinary collaboration can, however, provide maximum enlightenment. This sounds obvious, but is difficult to bring about in practice, whether in universities or out in the field, because of the blinkered attitudes of specialists to disciplines other than their own (this doubtless applies to archaeologists too).

We could imagine in an ideal world an expedition to the highlands of New Guinea, consisting of a social and a physical anthropologist, other social scientists, a linguist, an archaeologist and other scientists concerned with the environment and natural resources. (The role here of the ethnographer/ethnoarchaeologist will be discussed more fully in chapter 6.)

Archaeological evidence, in both its buried and above-ground elements, has a great variety of sources. These range from small artefacts (such as a pin) to major structures (such as the Taj Mahal or Stonehenge), together with the landscapes in which they are found or survive. Numerous disciplines lend their assistance both to the discovery of this diverse material and to its full understanding. The material, and the patterns which can be discerned across space and time, become the archaeological evidence, which may then be made relevant by describing and explaining it. The social, economic and religious framework are the *systems* of society whose interaction must be understood in the context of total history (figures 1 and 2).

Archaeology may thus be seen as a separate discipline, with its own approaches and methods, heavily dependent on the help of many specialists, but having the special aim of understanding a very long time-span in diverse habitats. Since his or her interest extends well before the period for which other sources are available, the archaeologist is interested not only in important events, such as those recorded in written documents, but in the whole fabric of society, from the activities of hunter-gatherers to those of town dwellers, from peasants to chieftains, from lakeside villagers to those in desert areas. Archaeology is mostly impersonal, concerned with societies and trends rather than individual people.

# ARCHAEOLOGY
## and OTHER SUBJECTS

*Resources :*   WATER

SOIL *( pedology )*

ROCKS *(geology )*

POWER ~ gravity,wind,water,solar , fire *(technology)*

WOOD and other plants *( botany )*

ANIMALS ~ land and sea *(zoology etc. )*

*Techniques :*  DEVELOPMENT OF THEORY *(philosophy )*

PROSPECTING , DISCOVERY *(geophysics , chemistry )*

IDENTIFICATION and ANALYSIS *(geology,
chemistry, botany, zoology etc., metallurgy)*

DATING *(physics,chemistry, geology, botany )*

STATISTICS, PATTERNING, ORIENTATION etc.
*(mathematics, computing, astronomy )*

*Artefacts and other residues ( below and above ground)*

FOOD, MEDICINE *( zoology, botany )*

TOOLS,CONTAINERS,WEAPONS, BUILDINGS,
VEHICLES, FURNITURE,CLOTHING,JEWELLERY,etc.
*(geology,metallurgy, botany, zoology, technology )*

COINS *(numismatics )*

RITUAL OBJECTS *(anthropology, theology )*

MUSICAL INSTRUMENTS *(musicology )*

ART *(art-history )*

MAPS *(cartography )*

INSCRIPTIONS *(epigraphy )*

DOCUMENTS *(history )*

HUMAN and ANIMAL REMAINS
*(human biology, zoology, etc. )*

## *INTERDISCIPLINARY COLLABORATION*

*Figure 2* The relationship of archaeology and other subjects

### THE LIMITATIONS OF ARCHAEOLOGY AND
### HOW TO OVERCOME THEM

To those who are not interested in archaeology, it appears to have two major limitations. Firstly, it is rarely concerned with named people. Non-archaeologists *like* names, and the interest of many people in their past rarely extends beyond such real or imaginary characters as Julius Caesar or King Arthur. Secondly, it fails to satisfy those who are primarily interested in the working of the human mind. These limitations of archaeology are at the root of many of the problems discussed in later chapters.

It must be said, in the final part of this chapter, that archaeologists themselves have become increasingly dissatisfied with these limitations to their understanding of the past, and have sought ways, by improving theory or technique, to overcome them. These attempts have dominated the recent history of archaeology, and may be summarized here briefly. In the short history of the subject (a century or two at most; Daniel, 1975) the ambitions of archaeologists began with the collection, description and classification of artefacts and buildings; graduated to the delineation of past lifestyles and technological and economic systems; and finally went on to much more ambitious aims. One of these aims was to understand not just the past of human beings, but also the environment they have evolved in, reacted to and adapted where possible.

There are two schools of thought here: the first, to which I personally subscribe, is that all human achievements are wholly the result of interaction with the environment. 'Control' of the environment by altering it has led to a massive if temporary increase in population, and an expansion into relatively hostile areas of the world. This may in the long run prove to be disastrous. Hominids could prove to be a relatively short-lived species compared to other life-forms, such as bees, dinosaurs etc. This may in the event be seen as merely another example of the working of natural selection.

The second school of thought in this debate opposes such 'environmental determinism', a concept which was widely promoted in the 1960s, but appeared to its opponents to denigrate human achievements and to relegate the human being to the status of 'just another animal'. This doesn't worry me personally; animals are just different in some ways. A characteristic of many human beings is, however, that they feel superior to other life-forms; and, with few exceptions, they are prepared to exploit them in the service of humans. This attitude is still prevalent, but there are indications of a change of heart about animal rights. The Archbishop of York, Dr John Habgood, who on his accession to the archdiocese supported medical experimentation on animals, has recently (during a service in Westminster Abbey to celebrate the 150th anniversary of the RSPCA, October 1990) deplored such cruelty and arrogance, and even referred to animals as 'our brothers and sisters'.

Another major change in attitude resulted from a revolution in the theory of archaeology – the so-called 'New Archaeology'. This was influential on both sides of the Atlantic, and gained many supporters in the 1960s and 1970s. There were many facets to this movement, one of which was an emphasis on model building and hypothesis testing. This was in contrast to what archaeologists of my generation had all been brought up to do: that is, to assemble the data and try to see what they added up to. The new approach was more formal. A model or hypothesis of what a past society might have been like is set up; and the question is then asked, 'What archaeological evidence would support or refute the model?' The archaeologist then designs a research strategy which will provide the kinds of data relevant to the model, and (as a corollary) pays less attention to that which is not relevant to the enquiry.

Another facet of the 'New Archaeology' was the adoption of a 'systemic approach', in which all the 'systems' operating in a society were considered individually and in interaction with others. Such systems would include the environment, subsistence, craft and technology, social hierarchy and ideology (religion, burial etc.). This amounts to a study of the complex ways in which human society changes through time. Such an approach is illustrated in relation to Wharram Percy in figure 7, and discussed on page 155.

The study of the environment had, however, an important

role in a systemic approach (figure 1). This was made more effective in the 1970s by dramatic developments in the natural sciences, notably in dating and microscopic analysis. Archaeology became more scientific; it was partly this that brought about a major reaction against the new archaeology, again because it allowed little scope for the contribution of the individual, and especially for that of the human mind.

Trends in archaeological theory in the 1980s followed the influence of structuralism in the arts and social sciences. 'Structures in the human mind' and symbolism in archaeological interpretation have become potent. Some archaeologists (notably Ian Hodder at Cambridge; Hodder, 1982, and later books) believe that human minds have a far greater importance in the development of society than what these archaeologists see as rather mundane factors of climate, environment and economic or political necessity. The effect of the mind on material remains is of course difficult to gauge from merely examining, for example, patterns on pottery. It can only shown by ethnoarchaeology. An archaeologist may go and live in an African village. Such an observer may see pottery being made and decorated. If he or she is a competent linguist, it may be possible to discern what people are thinking, what social tensions exist, what group allegiances or feuds are going on. Linking these together, it may be possible to see that patterns on pottery have little to do with regional style, religious belief or custom, but depend on whether, for instance, the female potter is attempting to assert her independence from her stepmother.

Contemporary trends towards such a 'cognitive' approach are ambitious and interesting, and at least alert the more traditional archaeologist to a wider range of explanation than has hitherto been assumed, in attempts to understand human behaviour from material remains.

I am not personally sympathetic to these current trends. I deplore the tendency to personalize archaeology, as will I hope be apparent throughout this book. What really interests me as an archaeologist is the whole working out of human destiny on the broadest possible canvas, in its interaction with genetic background, environment and all other life-forms.

This has been a rather heavy discussion, which it is impossible to do justice to in a book of this kind. For a fuller exposition of my philosophy in these matters, the reader is referred to my paper on 'Decision-making in the Past' (Rahtz, 1988b).

Archaeologists are not scientists in the textbook sense. One reason for this disclaimer is that much of the work they do, and the conclusions they come to, cannot be repeated or tested by someone else. The essence of a scientific experiment is that it can be done again and the same results achieved. This is obviously impossible in archaeology, especially in excavation, as the evidence is destroyed in the process of recovering it.

I spent two years excavating the Saxon and medieval palaces at Cheddar in Somerset; I recovered much evidence – post-holes of many great wooden buildings, details of numerous ditches, coins, pottery, metal objects and bones. From all these I wrote a report (Rahtz, 1979a) in which I tried to make sense of all this, working out what had happened at Cheddar between the ninth and fourteenth centuries AD. In particular, I split everything there into seven separate periods, which I thought represented significant episodes of building construction and activity – times when resources were put into development, in this case principally by the authority of kings or bishops. My seven phases are generally accepted as 'true'. They are, however, essentially *my* story, *my* ordering and interpretation of a very diverse and difficult body of evidence, recovered in a hurry, as the site was to be destroyed by the building of a school.

But what would another archaeologist have found? Unfortunately we shall never know – I can't put it all back so that someone else can repeat the experiment. The best we can do is to record as much as we can, and as objectively as possible. Anyone who has been on a dig knows how subjective most of the 'evidence' and what it 'means' is (see 'How likely is likely?' in chapter 7). We can only do out best by at least publishing full data, however subjective, which others can rework. Some well-recorded nineteenth-century excavations have been thus successfully reinterpreted in the light of modern ideas. In later generations, I hope that Cheddar can be rethought from *the data* I have published.

Even if we cannot claim to be scientists, we can try to be as

11

rigorous as possible, by enlisting various specialist skills. It is no good nowadays just recording that 'in this pit were ten Roman sherds and a lot of greenish dirt.' Scientists can describe the dirt accurately and suggest its derivation. Is it human or animal cess? Did it all get put in at once, or drift in very slowly? What is the exact composition of each sherd of pottery? What grits were used, how hot was the kiln?

At the very least, an archaeologist tries to argue the case objectively, and especially logically. What is the evidence, as far as it can be discerned? What hypothesis may be put up to explain its 'meaning'? How is this hypothesis to be tested? What alternative hypotheses can be put up, to be tested and possibly rejected in turn? Which seems on balance most likely? Having decided, this one doesn't become 'true'; archaeologists' evasiveness here causes much irritation to scientists and non-scientists alike.

Good archaeologists are logical in what they write in a report (in contrast to wild stories invented at tea-time on the dig), and also essentially rational. This engenders much enmity, because few people like rationality. In chapter 7 we shall meet some of these enemies, non-rationalists who are more interested in finding proof for their favourite theory about King Arthur, Atlantis or spacemen building stone circles. Rationalism is the enemy of romance, but to many people the past is, by definition, romantic. This is why archaeologists may find it difficult to sell 500 copies of a monograph representing several years of sustained hard work while Von Däniken can sell over forty million copies of *Chariots of the Gods?* (1989) and its sequels.

We shall also explore the major fallacy about finds. Most people are convinced that archaeologists dig for finds, preferably of gold or silver. Hence the metal detectors' claims that they can 'do archaeology' better than archaeologists. This is, alas, an attitude encouraged by museums (with notable exceptions) and by those who place cash value on archaeological artefacts.

While it is true that many rich and valuable finds, such as those from the tomb of Tutankhamun or Sutton Hoo (chapter 8), *are* also extremely important archaeologically, they are to an archaeologist only a means to an end, to understanding the human past, and not things to sell or put on shelves in a collection. To non-archaeologists they are also objects of beauty and rarity, which do have commerical value.

It is difficult to interest everybody in subjects like past economic systems, social structure or ancient environments. As we have already noted, people are interested in people, hence the appeal of *Neighbours* or *EastEnders*. It is sad that the skilful depictions of the associated social backgrounds in Sydney and London excite little comment.

A well-preserved body was found in a Cheshire peat-bog, dating from 2,000 years ago; he was at first called 'Lindow Man' after the name of the bog. It was a remarkable discovery, and a splendid opportunity to bring modern techniques to bear. An autopsy showed that the body was that of a healthy young man in his late twenties, with a fractured skull, broken ribs and a massive dislocation of the neck. His nails were carefully manicured, hinting at a person of noble birth. Violence was clearly the cause of death; so in this archaeological discovery there was the material for a whodunit. The public were, not surprisingly, intrigued at such details of a past *person*, so much more evocative than broken pottery or post-holes. So the scientific name of 'Lindow Man' gave way in the popular press to the vernacular 'Pete Marsh'.

Personalization, however, did not stop there. Analysis of the stomach contents (the remains of a burnt bannock or flat cake of unleavened barley) led to a theory that the man was ritually sacrificed on May Day in AD 60. This was to placate the gods after the disastrous spring of that year, in which the Celts suffered the loss of their most hallowed druidic stronghold on Anglesey and the crushing of Boudicca's rebellion. Going even further, he was now provided with a *real* name, as a druid called 'Lovernios', and was also proclaimed to be possibly a prince.

Summarized baldly like this, the identification sounds very far-fetched, and more the stuff of the lunatic fringe than archaeology. Yet the theory was in fact part-authored by one of the

13

most eminent Celtic scholars in Britain. In using the 'scientific facts' as 'the springboard for an imaginative leap into the unknown', Dr Anne Ross and her co-author Don Robins brought considerable scholarship to bear, and undoubtedly helped to popularize Lindow Man under his new name as a druid prince; and the book which developed this personalization is a best-seller (Robins and Ross, 1989).

This obsession with our own species as 'people' is known rudely as anthropocentrism. History is vastly more popular than archaeology because named people figure in it quite a lot; and not just any people, but 'interesting' ones like queens, generals, prime ministers, dictators and criminals. Most people in the past who made buildings and pottery, threw away rubbish and got buried in graves were none of these things. They were peasants, the submerged nine-tenths whose activities didn't hit the headlines of the Anglo-Saxon Chronicle, and whose very names are mostly unknown.

*All* people and their activities, their lives and their deaths, are the concern of the archaeologist, in efforts to understand the five-million year history of humankind. Sadly, to most people this is dull stuff, though I hope the reader will not be among them when he or she has read this book.

If archaeology is so dreary, unromantic, impersonal and rational, why do archaeologists like it? They are, after all, ordinary people. Who are they? How did they come to be interested? Who pays them to do it? In our next chapter we explore these questions.

# 2

# Motivation, Finance and Politics

There are many different kinds of archaeologist. They include the most abstruse theorists, concerned only with abstract ideas on the relationship between material residues and human behaviour; these are close to philosophers in their interests in the structure of knowledge. At the other end of the scale is the unemployed labourer working on an excavation. The best-known British archaeologist, the late Sir Mortimer Wheeler (Hawkes, 1982), asked one of the latter what he found most interesting in the work; the reply was, not surprisingly, 'the five o'clock whustle'! Academics think, do and teach archaeology, and provide the framework of learning and doing for graduate and undergraduate students (chapter 5). In Britain the total number of university lecturers who teach some archaeology is relatively small, no more than a few hundred. Other archaeologists are employed in fully professional units, such as those in York and London; each of these is currently working on a budget of up to a million pounds, and with a staff of a hundred or more. Archaeologists may work under the aegis of a university department such as that at Durham, or of a local goverment authority such as the unit at Carlisle.

In all cases much of the finance has in the past come from central government, but privatization is growing. It is increasingly expected that archaeologists will seek funds from private sponsors. These can be major institutions such as banks or mineral extraction companies, which are willing to fund archaeology as a cheap form of advertising. Some institutions like to improve their public image by a demonstration that they care about the cultural and artistic heritage – as with similar support for art, music or ballet.

There is also a growing lobby for the concept that 'the developer pays' – as with pollution. Building a multistorey hotel in a historic city like York will damage its environment; and it will also destroy the below-ground archaeology. Developers are expected to fund excavation; they are under pressure to do so from archaeologists, conservationists and local government planning authorities; such funding is also to a slight extent encouraged by national legislation. The developer is often prepared to go along with this (up to perhaps 1–2 per cent of the total building cost) to maintain a good public image.

In London especially there has evolved a developers' and archaeologists' code of practice. This defines the ways in which developers support archaeology in exchange for collaboration, especially in the avoidance of delay. This can be expensive. The discovery of the foundations of Shakespeare's Rose Theatre during building works in London in 1989 aroused great public interest; opposition to further construction work came not only from archaeologists, but more vociferously from famous actors, who organized pickets and sit-ins to stop the work proceeding. In the end a compromise was reached, and the remains of the theatre partly preserved; but the furore cost several million pounds. This sort of situation can be avoided by building archaeology into the planning process. In this case the presence of the theatre could have been foreseen, but contingency plans should also be made for really unexpected discoveries.

Major commercial developers and construction companies have on the whole been remarkably co-operative in allowing for the demands of archaeology, by giving either time, money or resources such as earth-moving machinery. The public sector is, however, less helpful. When a programme of major road improvement was announced in Britain, English Heritage made a survey of the number of sites likely to be damaged or destroyed, based on known data. They estimated that the archaeology of the roadworks would cost £73 million. In an intemperate outburst, the then Minister of Transport, Cecil Parkinson, retorted that this was sheer guesswork, and offered half-a-million pounds!

A further aspect of privatization is in archaeological units themselves. They were originally set up to cope with the needs of archaeology in cities like York, London or Oxford; but they have been forced by market pressures to be more entrepreneurial in order to maintain full employment for their staff. Thus we find the Birmingham Unit digging in Scarborough, and the Oxford Unit digging in Dover, London, Northamptonshire and Wiltshire; the range of their recent work is well demonstrated in *Current Archaeology*, **121** (October, 1990). Such activity is sometimes seen by local archaeologists as 'encroachment', and has led to some unpleasant confrontations and even legal proceedings.

In Western Europe there are major state or regional research institutes, such as the Dutch State Archaeological Service, or the province-based institutes in Spain or northwest Germany. These are more academically linked than those in Britain, and some are directly organized as part of university research, such as the Institute for Pre- and Proto-history at the University of Amsterdam. In Britain smaller numbers of professionals work in the Ordnance Survey, mapping antiquities; in the Royal Commission on Historical Monuments, recording landscapes, structures and buildings; and in English Heritage (the Historic Buildings and Monuments Commission), caring for our 'ancient monuments', which range from prehistoric earthworks to great castles, abbeys and historic houses. The staff of museums are employed principally in collecting, conserving and displaying the objects and results of archaeology; but some, such as the British Museum, sponsor or organize field-work in Britain or overseas; and many museums do employ full-time archaeologists to look after the archaeology of their local area.

European and North American countries have a reasonably large number of archaeologists investigating the past, though nothing like enough to care adequately for all the monuments or rescue evidence from those that have to be destroyed. Elsewhere in the world the situation is not so good, and in many places quite disastrous in under-provision. Mozambique, in southeast

Africa, has *two* archaeologists only, responsible for an area the size of Britain.

Apart from such people working in institutions, there are also professional freelance archaeologists, making a living from digging (as I did for ten years), lecturing on cruises, writing books, appearing on TV or radio and writing up the results of archaeological research. There is a growing number of such archaeologists working as consultants for local councils, developers, construction companies and insurance companies, as archaeological 'hazards' are taken more seriously and responsibly by those engaged in construction work.

Apart from those who do archaeology for money, there are also many amateurs. Their role and status (invaluable help or menace) varies from country to country. In Britain there is a very strong amateur tradition going back over a century to the founding of regional archaeological societies. They help on excavations, in museums and in field survey. For many their stimulus comes from attending extramural classes. Most are content to do routine work such as pot-washing, cataloguing or digging. They have, however, felt rather aggrieved at being denigrated to the status of dogsbodies to the professionals: used as 'trowel-fodder'. Many of them believe they have a crucial role to play in an economic situation where much archaeology is lost because the professionals cannot cope.

Some have higher aspirations, and there are a number whose work rates alongside that of academics or field professionals. Don Spratt, for instance, retired in his fifties from a post as research leader in ICI, enrolled at Sheffield University as a mature student, and went on to do important field-work in North Yorkshire and publish his results to the highest professional standards. The amateur involvement in Wharram Percy, in East Yorkshire, has been fundamental to its success, and will be more fully discussed in chapter 8. There is now a Council for Independent Archaeology, which exists to further the interests of amateurs in Britain, and provide them with expert services (see pages 170–1).

The range of people engaged in archaeology in other countries is similar to that in Britain, but certain differences will become apparent later in this chapter when we look at political and other motivations. In should be noted that archaeologists don't work only in their own countries. There are British schools or institutes in places such as Rome, Athens, Ankara and Jerusalem; and other countries, especially Germany, Italy, France and the USA, have mounted major expeditions abroad, notably in the fields of Greco-Roman and Holy Land archaeology. There is also 'colonial' archaeology, such as that of the French in Algeria and Tunisia, the English and French in Egypt when it was under Anglo-French mandate, and the English in India. These activities are in some places resented by indigenous archaeologists, who develop their own archaeology free from 'foreign' influence (see below, pages 29–30).

## WHY DO PEOPLE DO ARCHAEOLOGY?

Motivations are private and public, academic and commercial. I will list these, and then, in a brief world tour, see what is characteristic of different areas and (in chapter 3) how many apply in Britain. I have ranged them in an order of 'respectability' (ranging from the purely academic to the frankly sinister), but I do not expect my readers to agree with this ranking, which clearly reflects my own cultural prejudices.

(1) Intellectual curiosity: the pursuit of knowledge for its own sake. This aspiration has been characteristic of humans for many thousands of years at least, and is generally recognized as a valid approach, and one which should be supported by public and private funds. (It is, however, increasingly under insidious attack by governments and other institutions with an eye to short-term economic gain and 'social relevance'.) The latter can, though, be invoked where research is allied to anthropology, to help existing rather than dead peoples.

(2) The provision of data about the past to help us to predict and change the future. Can politicians learn from history or archaeology and avoid making the same mistakes? To paraphrase a well-

known quotation: 'the only thing we learn from archaeology is that people never learn anything from archaeology.'

(3) Public education: giving everybody a wider perspective of humankind's past, helping them to live in the world today, and at the least enriching their lives in their visits to ancient monuments and museums. This is the great 'cultural heritage' bandwagon on to which many archaeologists are now climbing.

(4) The promotion of tourism, with attendant financial gain; there is a grey area between this and (3) above. Tourist-related archaeology at its best can be highly educational, and it can present an authentic view of the past.

The Jorvik Viking Centre at York (see also page 168) has been visited by several million people. It recreates a Viking townscape with people; and everything visible to the public in their slowly moving 'time cars', as well as the sounds they hear and the foul smells around them, is evidenced by archaeology, history or language.

At Dover, the White Cliffs Experience (see also pages 168–9) uses similar high technology to tell the story of Dover through history, from the conquest of the Romans and their Channel Fleet (the *Classis Britannica*), complete with lighthouses, right through to Dover as a famous ferry-port, and as the British 'front line' during the Second World War, when it was heavily shelled by Germans from the other side of the Straits.

Such tourist-minded centres that are also highly educational to very large numbers of people are *the* principal means of bringing archaeology to the widest public, whether in museums, reconstructed buildings, cathedral treasuries or, best of all, the great folk-parks of Scandinavia, Ulster, Wales and the USA) Sturbridge Old Village, near Boston, Massachusetts, has a 20-ha site where we see an early nineteenth-century village in action, with church, mill, carpenter's shop, pottery kiln, farm, eating-house and church. Everyone is in costume, doing, making or serving. A shop sells all the things made in the village: you can furnish your home entirely in early Puritan style. Thirty-four staff are employed, including an archaeologist. The appeal is wide, satisfying the ordinary American in search of roots and nostalgia, and also the visiting foreign archaeologist interested in New England culture.

Such enterprises as Jorvik and Sturbridge were pioneers in what has now become a major growth area – the heritage industry (Hewison, 1987; and see pages 167–70). Tourism orientation is often excellent in its results, if not always in its motivation; at worst it can be highly misleading and a total rip-off.(Archaeology has to be cost-effective and money-spinning to survive) and this in England is the philosophy behind English Heritage. Our monuments should be made attractive, while hopefully avoiding scandals such as Stonehenge, where public car-parks, lavatories and wire disfigure the open landscape of Salisbury Plain, and where one cannot even touch the stones. The situation at this world-famous site is, however, improving; plans are in hand for the 1990s to make a new information centre, to close the road that passes the site and to make Stonehenge the great 'experience' it should be.

(5) The establishment of a common basis for humanity in the past. Present-day world society is highly diverse, culturally and linguistically, leaving aside the superficialities of colour and other characteristics which divide us. Archaeology can perhaps give us a better perspective, in showing that only a few hundred generations ago we were all hunter-gatherers with a common interest in staying alive and reproducing ourselves; these indeed remain our preoccupations in the late twentieth century. Can such a unity of interest be restored in the face of possible environmental disaster?

Some political use has been made of this concept in the USSR. The results of prehistoric research have been used in museums to emphasize that if one goes back far enough, the USSR was one society, not the separate racial, cultural and linguistic groups now asserting their independence of central authority.

(6) The definition and assertion of ethnic identity and cultural roots, or even (at worst) of ethnic superiority. This may be used either to create a national identity or to stimulate 'lost' national pride; or more aggressively to justify subjugation or colonization

of 'inferior' peoples – many examples will be cited later this chapter.

(7) The legitimization of male or female dominance or superiority. The ball has in the past been mainly in the male court – man as the food-hunter, the strong protector, the builder, the king, the pope and so on – but increasingly the results of ethnographic or archaeological research may be cited to support feminist claims that females are more crucial to the survival of the species. It is they who provide the *regular* food supply by gathering and later by farming (hunters often fail), who succour the children, who invent. Patriarchal, male-dominated societies may be a relatively recent phenomenon, and examples may be found of societies where women take on all the 'male' roles of politicians, land-owners, warriors, or priests.

(8) The accumulation of archaeological data to test hypotheses. It has been said that European-descended American archaeologists investigating American Indian archaeology in the USA do so not out of interest in the culture (and still less for the benefit of the culture's inheritors), but to provide fodder for computer analysis. They cannot identify with the people whose settlements and graves they are digging up; but Arkansas is nearer to home than Greece, where they'd *really* like to work if they had the money!

(9) The proving of the truth of myth by invoking the so-called 'evidence of archaeology'. This is something I have had direct experience of, having dug at Glastonbury for six seasons. The material under this heading is so rich as to be worth the full treatment it is going to get in chapter 7.

(10) The validation of religious belief. Mortimer Wheeler called Palestine 'the land of original archaeological sin', the implication being that much of what purported to be scientific archaeology, investigating the contexts of the Old and New Testaments, was not only bad archaeology, but grossly biased in its interpretation towards what the expedition or its sponsors wished to prove. Examples elsewhere are the expeditions to Mount Ararat in Tur-

key to find Noah's Ark, or the excavations at Tara in Ireland by
the British Israelites in 1912 to dig up the Ark of the Covenant.
In the latter case, enormous damage was done to one of Tara's
most important earthworks, which left very little for a later Irish
excavator.

(11) The establishment or maintenance of the ego of the individual. This has been my own primary motivation, and I suspect
not as absent from even the academic archaeological scene as we
would like to think. This is not perhaps as bad as it may sound (a
number of people were offended by this in the first edition of this
book). We all like to be admired and to have our achievements
recognized by society; and our efforts are often related to career
prospects.

Related to this is the promotion of the public image of institutions. This may be a matter of pride, or of securing financial
sponsorship; but it can sometimes lead to dubious ethical actions,
such as the buying of treasures looted from tombs or of other
unfortunate origin.

Slightly more respectable is the removal of objects to a 'safe'
place from some 'backward' country, which cannot look after its
cultural heritage. In the case of the Benin Bronzes, this was no
more than legalized looting from Nigeria; but Elgin did believe
he was saving the Parthenon marble frieze, and he was right,
insofar as the fragments in the British Museum are the only ones
which are now in good condition, Athenian pollution having
severely eroded the rest. He did also obtain them in an entirely
legal way. But now that the Greeks have proper conditions to
look after them, they are in my view justified in asking for them
back.

(12) The search for treasure or other loot, including art objects,
for the royal or aristocratic purse, or for the enrichment of
private or museum collection. This is a very ancient motivation,
going back in England to our medieval monarchs, who ordered
ancient burial mounds to be dug for the gold or treasures they
might contain.

Such seeking for finds in highly prevalent today all over the

23

world, sometimes done in ignorance (as with many metal-detector enthusiasts), but often with full cognizance of the damage done to sites, and robbing us of our cultural heritage for private profit or for social or institutional aggrandizement.

A WORLD TOUR

In this brief survey of case-studies of the good and bad motivations that inspire archaeology in various countries, we are examining principally *public* archaeology. By that I mean work which has been financed from public funds, and which has therefore been thought valid and useful to society by those who sign the cheques – the acid test of commitment to a cause. We shall see that the respectable and questionable motivations for archaeological work are both closely related to the history of each country, and the present political and religious beliefs of its leaders.

Archaeology in IRELAND is supported by the state and the universities, and tends to be nationalist in both cases. Archaeology at University College, Dublin, is taught in a Department of *Celtic* Archaeology. Up to a point the Republic has encouraged the pursuit of Irish Archaeology, that is to say *real* Irish archaeology, by which they meant pre-Viking. The Irish coinage is based on symbols of their early culture (wolfhound, bear, harp etc.) In Dublin the internationally important excavations of the rich Viking urban levels were starved of resources; much that was bulldozed away was as archaeologically rich and well preserved as the famous Viking dig of Coppergate in York. The director of the excavations appealed for more funds to his employers, the National Museum. The discouraging reply, with a sad smile, was 'Ah now, if only it were Early Christian!' Much passion and rancour was generated by later legal battles, resulting in a bout of fisticuffs outside the court between two very eminent archaeologists, one Irish, the other English.

These biases are also responsible for the concentration in Irish archaeology on what the late Michael O'Kelly (then Professor of Archaeology at the University of Cork) use to call 'all those squiggles'. 'Squiggle archaeology' was concerned with Irish Christian art – high crosses, religious and other remains of Ireland's Golden Age. The discovery by a metal detector, illicitly digging on an Irish monastic site, of the Derrynaflan Early Christian treasure was hailed by the National Museum (but not by other responsible people in Ireland) as a great and important discovery for the nation.

Academic life does not escape current politics in the secular sphere. Peter Fowler and I gave papers at a prestigious Irish conference, but we had to leave a reception hastily when the president of the sponsoring academic organization said in a loud voice that 'the only Englishmen whom he could tolerate were those through whom he could see daylight'; we retreated from a fight on that occasion.

The political use of archaeology by Nazi GERMANY, notably by the use of the writings of the archaeologist Gustav Kossina, is well known (Renfrew, 1973). The aim was to establish Aryan racial supremacy and the inferiority of the Slavs. 'From Germany spread megalithic cultures of Indo-Germans; flint daggers were glorified as evidence of a noble pride and joy in weapons; the trumpets of the Nordic Bronze Age were evidence of German superiority in music already in prehistoric times, contrasting their majestic volume combined with gentleness with the monotone diatonic melodies of the south' (quoted in Clark, 1965, page 260). German archaeology has, fortunately, totally recovered its high position in European archaeology, with very large and efficient excavations and scholarship of the highest academic standard. Some of the most important work in Germany has been on the early medieval period. This is because this was one of the high points of German civilization; the fifth and sixth centuries are when German culture was exported (at sword-point) to revitalize the decadent Latin culture of the Roman Empire (and hence the English!).

Each country takes pride in its Golden Age, and this is reflected in its archaeology and museum display. In SCANDINAVIA the Swedes show the rich remains of their seventh-century Vendel and Valsgärde cultures, pre-Viking and contemporary with Sutton Hoo (chapter 8). The Norwegians, on the other hand, are proud of their Viking past. At Oslo there is a magnificent ship-museum of this age, and it was of course a Norwegian who sailed a Viking replica ship across the Atlantic in 1893; it was a Norwegian who, in 1978, with his 13-year-old daughter, rowed across the North Sea, and up the River Ouse to York, possibly to reclaim the lost kingdom of Eric Blood-Axe. Denmark has enormous public support for archaeology. Its popular magazine, *Skalk*, has a circulation of over 50,000, forty times that of its English equivalent per head of the population. Their prehistory and Vikings are equally popular. It was their Bronze Age trumpets (*lurs*) which gave the name to Lurpak butter.

Millions of pounds were spent, over a period of a quarter of a century, in raising the *Wasa* from the seabed in the harbour of Stockholm, and conserving it. This was a seventeenth-century battleship, the pride of the Swedish navy, which, however, sank within hours of its launching. It was a fine ship, and a reminder of a great period in Swedish naval history; it has now been dried out and made the centrepiece of a magnificent museum in Stockholm.

In the NETHERLANDS the Dutch destroyed much of their medieval heritage in their Golden Age of the seventeenth century, but we are left with the glories of the new work in places like Amsterdam, Leiden and Delft. Holland is one of the few places where, in the course of several tours, I have detected no motivation that was not of the most impeccable academic order, whether by state or by university.

I have already mentioned RUSSIA'S (possibly now vain) attempt to stress the essential prehistoric unity of widely distant areas of the USSR. Nationalism, however, plays an important role in decision making in the financing of public archaeology. One of the most long-drawn-out disputes in the interpretation of archaeological finds centres on the area around Lake Ladoga. Here there are rich cemeteries with Swedish-made swords. To the Swedes, these are evidence of the graves of aristocratic or entrepreneurial merchants who had penetrated the river-systems. These merchants, the *Rus* or Eastern Vikings, went on eventually to the glories of Byzantium, and their enrolment in the crack

Varangian Guard there. To the Russians, however, these weapons belonged to the indigenous Slavic people, who by means of *their* mercantile genius had developed the economy, markets and wealth that made them able to buy this prestigious equipment.

It was nationalism too which led to the financing of massive excavations in Novgorod, dear to Russian hearts as the predecessor of Moscow before the fifteenth century, and the symbol of 'old Mother Russia' (Mongait, 1961).

We know very little of the important archaeology of CHINA. For a long time it was the preserve of foreign scholars, who experienced difficulties. Archaeology was, in the peasants' view, unpropitious, 'jarring the susceptibilities of the spirits and interfering with fertility' (Clark, 1965, page 258). After the revolution, archaeology was taken up in a big way by the communist state as a major tool in inculcating pride, not only in China's past, but in the earlier achievements of the workers.

A major revelation in Britain was the 'Genius of China' Exhibition, displayed at the Royal Academy in London. There was a dazzling display of treasure of superb artistic quality, including the famous suit for the corpse of a princess, made of jade plaques. The message of the text of the guide, in spite of some editing in translation, came through loud and clear. There was primacy of invention (notably of metal-working); but what was most impressive was the justification for the excavation of rich aristocratic tombs rather than prehistoric peasant settlements. 'These amazing finds', ran the blurb, 'were made by the ordinary people, the artisans, working for their effete lords. Now they are being excavated and restored to the Chinese people who made them' (that is, by display in the museums of the Chinese People's Republic).

Fagan (1978) supplies further telling quotes from Chinese publications. 'Archaeology is used to underscore the suffering of workers in pre-revolutionary society.' 'Textile imports found in ancient cemeteries are evidence that China has always been interested in friendly Chinese neighbours.' 'The archaeological work at Lui Sheng's tomb of *c.*113 BC ... has mercilessly expressed the limits and extravagance of the aristocrats, as well as their brutal exploitation and oppression of the workers.' 'Her

27

suits had 2,690 pieces of jade and 38,025 length of gold thread; all
that remained of Lui Sheng were teeth' ... 'by destroying their
bodies, history has exacted a just retribution.' 'Lady Tai ... died
of heart failure and gallstones ... she was well-nourished, with
much subcutaneous fat.' 'She had led', said the doctor, 'the idle
dissipated life of the exploiting class.' As Chairman Mao said, 'let
the past serve the present.'

All emergent nations, shaking off the shackles of imperialist
domination, have used archaeology to develop and strengthen
ancient roots and establish the new state on a consciousness of the
great past. GHANA took its name from a medieval state further
inland, which is not even in the area of the new state (it is what is
now Mali). The most remarkable example is ZIMBABWE. The
name is that of an outstanding site where there are seven square
kilometres of extensive and massive stone buildings, witness to a
very well-organized and technically competent earlier society.

White racial prejudice would not allow that Great Zimbabwe
had been built by indigenous Africans; it was said that it must
have been the work of whites, whose presumed identity ranged
from the Queen of Sheba to early Portuguese merchants. It was,
however, the work of white archaeologists less hostile to black
aspirations which demonstrated beyond doubt that the site was
earlier than European influence, and that its material culture was
wholly indigenous. This demonstration of a former greatness
made Zimbabwe the symbol of the new country and gave it its
1980 name, helped by the fact that President Robert Mugabe
came from that area. The ruins have now been 'reclaimed' by
local people who leave offerings of goats and meat on the site
(BBC talk, 1983). Other monuments such as the European forts
are being 'de-proclaimed' as ancient sites, since they are, according to the African spokesman, 'blatantly colonial – monuments
of conquest'.

While African monuments such as Great Zimbabwe have become symbols of national identity, this very desire for nation-
hood is not consistent with the preservation of the local
cultural heritage. Peter Ucko, now professor of archaeology at
Southamptom, was invited by the British Council to 'evaluate
cultural awareness' in different parts of Zimbabwe, and assess the

viability of developing a kind of museum to be called 'local culture houses'. These would attempt to preserve the material cultural heritage of local ethnic, linguistic or cultural groups. Objects of special value, including especially items of spiritual or 'ritual' significance, would be in a locked room, but there would be more open areas with examples of arts and crafts (with direct sales to purchasers of items currently being made), taped oral histories and autobiographies.

While local peoples were strongly in favour of the development of culture houses, Ucko's report met with no support from the Zimbabwe government: 'archaeology could not be allowed to fuel the fires of potential rebellion'; the proposals smacked of 'tribalism' – a dirty word in an emergent nation. 'We must lose our ethnic identities in order to find our true selves within the context of Zimbabwean identity'; 'by the time our children leave secondary school, they should simply regard themselves as Zimbabweans irrespective of their tribal, regional or racial origins' (quotations from two Zimbabwe newspapers in May/June, 1981). Ucko's report was suppressed by both the British Council *and* the Zimbabwe government, and it was never published.

One major problem in African archaeology is to persuade Africans to be their own archaeologists. In emergent nations educated young people seek a higher status in society, such as that afforded by being a lawyer.

Nationalism is also a major factor in developing the archaeology of any nation which has a 'glorious' past. In ITALY, the Roman past hardly needed stressing: Rome is substantially Roman. Mussolini, however, capitalized on this, pouring money into the uncovering of more and more monuments, and adopting the symbol of the *fasces* as his own. This was the symbol of the *lictors*, the chief Roman officials of law and order, and hence, for Mussolini, it became the symbol of order, discipline and authority, as much as of Rome itself. *Senatus populusque Romanus* finds its echo in the SPQR on manhole covers and other public utilities in Rome (these are coveted by my son, whose names are Sebastian Patrick Quintus). Italy also provides us with an example of 'religious' archaeology. The Vatican sponsored excavations under St Peter's in the hope of discovering the tomb of St Peter;

not surprisingly the published work leans over-heavily to a positive interpretation of the results. Credibility would have been higher if the archaeologists responsible for the work had not been Roman Catholic priests.

Religion and nationalism came together in ISRAEL. It was a military commando who was also an archaeologist, Yigael Yadin, who was given enormous resources to dig Masada, the scene of the self-immolation of the Jews under Roman government. The rocky fortress is a potent symbol of Zionism today, visited by numerous tourists and school parties, almost as a pilgrimage.

In YUGOSLAVIA, the late Marshal Tito also had the task, after the Second World War, of merging diverse ethnic and cultural groups into a single state, now in danger of disintegrating. Archaeology has not, however, been used either to cement the unity of the whole country, or to validate local aspirations to independence. The main motive in sponsoring excavations is financial – the promotion of tourism. I worked on an American/ Yugoslav excavation on Diocletian's Palace at Split. The whole aim was not the understanding of the palace's remarkable urban continuity from the fourth century to the present day. Medieval levels were swept away, the object being to uncover Roman structures and mosaics and rich finds. The structures uncovered were rapidly consolidated and incorporated into new cafés. Hundreds of tons of stratified archaeological deposits were removed from the deep cellar-basements of the palace to allow them to be opened to public view. The 'dirt' was passed out along conveyor belts; anything 'important' such as statues, was picked off, and the rest was dumped in the sea.

Archaeology in Islamic countries is geared to the Islamic revolution. In IRAN, non-Islamic (Persian) monuments were severely damaged in the early excesses of the revolution. In LIBYA, Colonel Ghadafi is personally interested in archaeology – of a certain kind. I was invited to take over the excavations at Surt, a coastal town in the Libyan Gulf. This is a place of early medieval origin, not Roman, and as such owed its early importance to the growth of Islam as a trading centre of the eastern Mediterranean. I expressed an interest, keen to extend my urban and cultural experience, and involve my department in Mediterranean medieval archaeology. A research strategy was devised which would examine the town and its hinterland in a way which would define its natural resources, its origins, its town plan, the functions of its different areas, its trading connections and its economy – all standard objectives in modern urban studies. We were, however, over-optimistic in believing that the results would be of great interest to a modern Islamic state interested in its past. Colonel Ghadafi made his objection very clear. He was not interested in such a theoretical approach; what he wanted was someone who could uncover mosques and mosaics, and recover fine glass and ceramics, which would, in his view, redound more to the glory of Islam than to the aims of modern archaeology.

In MOROCCO, the great monuments of Islam, the palaces, mausolea and mosques of the former dynasties, are religious monuments, which are visited by Europeans as a tourist concession. Moulay-Idriss was the nucleus of the Islamic political and military conquest of the area (hence its proximity to the former Roman city, now the ruins, of Volubilis). In the eighth century, however, it became the centre for the Islamic faith. From then on, its political importance waned in favour of Fez, Rabat, Meknes and other dynastic centres, and it became a holy city, the 'poor man's Mecca' for those whose resources did not allow the long trip to Saudi Arabia. Since the modern Islamic revolution, Moulay-Idriss is closed at times to non-Islamic tourists. One has to go to Spain to see Islamic monuments in all their glory, as secular tourist attractions, at Granada or Córdoba.

Independence movements can also seek the support of archaeology in rather curious ways. That in the CANARIES, although instigated by secessionist Spaniards, has as its graffito-message *Guanche Independencia*. The Guanche were the indigenous inhabitants of the Canaries, probably of Berber origin, who are represented in archaeology by stone tools, rock paintings and tombs. They put up a surprising and long-drawn-out resistance to Iberian *conquistadores*.

In the past, archaeologists, along with soldiers, merchants, missionaries and anthropologists, were the agents and supporters of colonial oppression, studying 'primitive' peoples as inferior to

31

whites, but possibly as throwing some light on the life of our own 'barbarous' ancestors. Anthropologists have learnt their lesson here and abandoned their patronizing stance. In order to study other living societies, they have to adopt a posture of 'we are here to learn from you – our society is decadent and we have valuable lessons to learn.' They have also to bear with the inhabitants' aspirations of becoming westernized (oddly, the indigenes don't believe all these stories about how awful life is in the USA or Western Europe), and in the process they see them lose those cultural characteristics which make them an invaluable source for the study of the origins of humankind. The people also demand a share in the profits of any book or film which may be made of their activities. Anthropologists are now, together with archaeologists, firm anti-imperialists; as we have already seen in the case of Zimbabwe, the latter can provide valuable ammunition in the fight for independence. They can show, for instance, that American Indians in the USA or Aborigines in Australia have occupied the land for very long periods, of up to 40,000 years or more. This destroyed the claims of white colonialists that the indigenous people had not been there very long and that dispossession was wholly justified in terms of developing resources. Archaeologists can show the antiquity not only of humans, in those areas, but of cultural and ethnic groupings; and notably the antiquity of cemeteries. Their evidence has become increasingly important in re-establishing rights to land, and in re-ratifying former treaties.

Archaeologists have made direct contributions to the development of Third World countries by the improvement of living standards. Jean Gimpel has attempted to reintroduce simple 'lost technologies'; advanced machinery imported from the West is unsuitable because cost and maintenance requirements exceed local skills and reserves. For instance, the simple horizontal-wheeled watermill (one of my own areas of research – chapter 6) is being introduced into India and Africa by means of scale model demonstrations. In South America, Inca irrigation systems have been excavated and re-used.

In Northern CANADA, the indigenous Inuit Eskimos came into conflict with modern developers who wanted to build a large hydroelectric complex (*The Times*, 20 February 1982). This would have had a deleterious effect on their traditional hunting and fishing territories. The Inuits and Crees, assisted by sympathetic Canadians, stopped the project. A year later, an agreement was signed by all parties, making sure that future projects took all ecological needs into account. The associated reaseach is of great interest in demonstrating to archaeologists possible factors to take into account when interpreting the life of early hunter-gatherers in the north.

In modern AUSTRALIA, sometimes known as the 'fourth world', the Aborigines have all but lost their former way of life. For long despised as, abbos', these indigenous people fell victim to exploitation, degradation and extermination. Archaeology has shown that they can claim to be the most successful human beings in the world, having achieved a stable and balanced society in a hostile environment for forty millennia. Not many Australians believe this. When I expounded this view to a highly educated Australian postgraduate at York, her face exhibited utmost horror at this heresy. She gasped out, 'but they're just *animals*', and our conversation closed.

Some anthropological work was done in Australia in the post-war decades but, in common with all such researches, little attention was paid to material culture; emphasis was on societal institutions, kinship, inheritance and other related topics. It was only in recent years that archaeologists began to record the technical aspects of aboriginal culture. Some Aborigines have tried to return to their former lifestyle by going into the outback. They did not wish to relinquish wholly the efficient tools of the whites. Apart from steel knives and rifles, they wanted to take with them tape-recorders. This they saw as an invaluable way was not only of recording their folklore from an ever-diminishing number of old people, but of making sure it would never again be lost. Other Aborigines have been to the Australian Museum at Sydney to find out the uses of various tools, and the meaning of symbols. The museum staff help Aborigines who are seeking to re-establish their cultural identity. Some archaeologists become champions of aspirations to recover lost status; many become involved in saving important aboriginal sacred sites from flooding (by a proposed Tasmanian dam), exploitation or tourism. It was an encouraging victory when Ayers Rock was restored to the Aborigines as one of their most important religious sites. Archaeological work of a high order on the part of academics of Sydney and Canberra has shown the antiquity of the Aborigines, but too late to save them.

This might sound as if the archaeologists were the friends of the Aborigines. This is what the white archaeologists may have felt or intended, but that is not the way that they appeared to the Aborigines. Peter Ucko describes how they burst into tears when they see archaeologists at work, because of the disturbance of the natural world, created by their ancestors. Archaeologists were seen as 'disturbers of peace and religion'. They were 'the whites who dig holes that don't produce out of them either water or minerals which will bring us royalties'. Especially abhorrent to the Aborigines is the excavation of human remains: 'the archaeologists are the whites who disturb our ancestors to show we've been here for 40,000 years, but we know already, we've always been here since the dreamtime.' They are neither impressed by, nor interested in, radiocarbon dating (Ucko, 1983a, 1983b). Relationships were, however, improved when the Land Rights Act enabled the Aborigines to lay claim to land if they could show that they 'belonged there, owned it, and by kinship had always been there'. Archaeologists and anthropologists ceased to be the enemy, because they alone could (in theory) prove this longevity of occupation. Relationships changed from confrontation (sometimes at gun-point) to collaboration; by a *political* circumstance, archaeology was saved.

Another problem in Australian archaeology has been the definition and preservation of precolonial monuments. To the Aborigines, the important places may be natural features such as Ayers Rock, or particular localities. These are important to them as places to keep free of modern development (and from the taints of tourism). This cuts little ice with the whites, however, who can only see ancient monuments as things made by human beings which you can go and gape at. In Australia, this means especially rock paintings, which may date from many thousands of years ago or from more recent times. Australian governments, by attempting to preserve these, are imposing their own cultural viewpoint on the need to preserve the heritage, taking little notice of the interests of the indigenous minority. This now numbers between a quarter and half a million, depending on how an Aborigine is defined, or 1–2 per cent of the total population. Many Aborigines live in cities, and have vehicles, guns and other 'amenities' of white life. The only benefit *they* get from the preservation of rock paintings is the profits of tourist exploitation, where they can, with the help of the archaeologist, lay a claim to ownership.

Attempts have been made to 'educate' the Aborigines into an understanding of their own archaeology in scientific rather than dreamtime terms. They are increasingly represented on committees concerned with their own affairs, and offered help in attempts to preserve their cultural heritage for posterity. On hearing of these opportunities, an 84-year-old man applied to be taught how to dive. One of his ancestors had in dreamtime walked on the water across a strait; his footprints were believed to be preserved in the seabed, and the Aborigine wished to record them for posterity.

Australia is an excellent example of the problems of studying the past of people who are still around. While intelligent consideration of their interests and grasp of their culture may vastly increase our understanding of their archaeology, white archaeologists have until recently treated precolonial archaeology as if it were that of a dead people, as is done in Europe. In terms of social relevance, the fruits of archaeology are for the benefit of the wider public. In Australia there must surely be especial consideration given to providing the Aborigines with an archaeology not based on Eurocentric concepts, but with one appropriate to aboriginal interests.

Especially irrelevant is our concept of *time*, divided into calendar years, days, hours and minutes. While this may be necessary for the orderly running of modern capitalist societies, it is of little interest to those who have no calendars or clocks. To them, there are three kinds of past time: the immediate past of personal memory – the 'moving present'; the handed-on memories of one or two past generations; and ancestral time, While to the Aborigines these

35

divisions have a meaning at one level, at another they are all
the same – all coexisting in different planes. As archaeologists,
we should perhaps bear this in mind when interpreting the material residues of past societies.

Peter Ucko suggests that we should be less arrogant not only
in our relationships with Aborigines, but also in attempting to
promote archaeology to our own people. Even in England the
majority of people have no conception of a past measured in
millennia and centuries.

Similar problems exist in NEW ZEALAND: here archaeological remains are (apart from 'historical' European sites of
the eighteenth and nineteenth centuries) of only one culture, the
Maori. They are also of relatively recent date, New Zealand
having been colonized from Polynesia only about a thousand
years ago. When the first settlers found a fauna wholly unused to
human predators, life was easy. Maori archaeology is of the
greatest interest; earthworks and settlement sites abound, including lots of hillforts similar to those of our own European Iron
Age. Scholars have taken a keen interest in their archaeology.

Here also there have been clashes of interest concerning
ownership of sacred areas of land, and attempts to preserve
Maori culture and language. Far from being a potentially dying
indigenous minority, Maoris, after being decimated by white
exploitation and disease, have recently doubled in number and
have become highly vociferous and politically effective in securing their legal rights. They want nothing less than a bicultural
and bilingual society, with Europeans learning Maori. The indigenous cultural heritage is clearly in safe hands, and it will be
interesting to see how this affects Maori archaeology, and their
own participation in their past. A full understanding of Maori
archaeology does demand a full integration of surviving folklore,
ethnography and traditional history. The Maori are understandably reluctant to divulge all their secrets and religious beliefs. It is
said that in order to study Maori archaeology properly, one has
to marry a Maori.

We may next look at the UNITED STATES OF AMERICA.
We will first consider the archaeology of the indigenous Indian.
American Indian culture and most of the people have been des-

troyed in ways which are remarkably familiar to us from hundreds of films, and degraded into tourist-souvenir reservations. Their monuments get little better shrift. In New York state, I photographed two plaques which were meant to draw the publics's attention to 'archaeological' monuments. One, close to an American Indian settlement, is in the form of a white Christian cross, with a metal plate which reads:

### GANNAGARD

Largest of the Genesa Indian villages, was located on Boughton Hill. Rev J. ... C. ... preached and baptised here in 1677. The place was also visited by Rev J. ... G. ... and other Jesuit Missionaries. Rev J. ... G. ... had chapel and resided here in 1676–1677.

The place was destroyed by de Nonville's army in 1687 and the inhabitants driven eastwards.

I was warned not to attempt to look at the site of the village, as there was a rather unfriendly Indian living there who had a shotgun!

Another plaque, in the small town of Victor nearby, was made of metal. Surmounting it was a low relief depiction of an Indian chief complete with archetypal headdress, and a Christian cross hung round his neck. The text below ran:

In Perpetuation of the name of
### ATHASATA (KRYN)

The Great Christian Mohawk Chief, Promoter of Peace, respecter of treaties, defender of righteousness, valiant warrior, leader of Indian forces forming one third of the army of the de Nonville expedition, which *passed* (1687) *along the Indian trail.* [my italics]

'I cannot speak too highly of the assistance we received from the great Mohawk and his warriors: Our Christian Indians surpassed all, and performed deeds of valor, especially the Iroquois, upon which we had not dared to rely to fight against their relatives'. (de Nonville)

37

> The name of ATHASATA merits a place in history be-
> side the great Iroquois leaders.

– and we might add, alongside notable traitors elsewhere. What
is surprising about these notices is that they were erected in
relatively modern times, but do not appear to be embarrassing to
the present community.

Fortunately, the tide is turning. The present generation of
younger 'enlightened' American archaeologists *is* interested in the
American Indians, not only as a series of remarkable groups
in themselves, but also in their aspirations to social justice. As in
Australia, the demonstration by archaeologists of the 40,000-year
antiquity of the American Indians, and of their use of local
resources over very long periods, has done much to offset claims
that the 'recently-arrived' Indians had no better claim to the land
and minerals than the invading whites. Archaeological evidence
is brought to bear in law courts in support of modern Indians'
claims to land and the honouring of long-dishonoured treaties.

Secondly we may look at white Americans' culture. They do,
of course, suffer from an inferiority complex about their slight
antiquity. Some seek desperately to show that America was
visited or even colonized long before Columbus (see chapter 7).
Others are inspired by nationalism to study the times of the
pioneer settlements and the revolution, the war against the British. This is their historical archaeology – the excavation, and
study from documents, of eighteenth – and nineteenth – century
frontier forts, trading stations and early towns such as Williams-
burg. To us this seems all a bit recent, but not to white Americans. The work in this field is, however, of the greatest interest,
not only because of the opportunity to relate surviving material
culture to plentiful written sources, but because of the use made
of this data by New World archaeologists to develop archaeological theory.

These are wholly academic studies of a high order, yet they
also serve a nationalistic sentiment. The 'ancient monuments'
of Boston are the 'freedom trail' – the places where Bostonians
rebelled against the English, culminating in the 'tea party'. At

Marblehead, Massachusetts, the 'Old Burial Hill', where there is a fine collection of early gravestones, is marked by a plaque:

1630–1930
Established in 1638, one of the oldest graveyards in New England. Site of first meeting-house, *six hundred revolutionary heroes* and several early pastors were interred at the top of the hill. [my italics]

It is the revolution, rather than the early settlers, which is the dominant attraction of this archaeology.

An interesting question of wide relevance is the extent to which political ideologies affect not only the promotion of archaeology and its interpretation, but also the universal interpretation and synthesis on an academic level. Marxism, for instance, has up to recently provided a dominating interpretative framework for the past, not only for the archaeology of the USSR and other Eastern European areas, but also for Marxist historians and archaeologists everywhere. The class struggle and the control of the means of production are seen by them as the major explanatory factors in the development of all human societies from the Palaeolithic onwards.

Nor can archaeology escape the pressures of modern politics. In Britain, archaeology was the first academic discipline to be involved in the 'academic freedom' debate in relation to South Africa and apartheid. In 1986, the World Archaeological Congress met in Southampton. Following pressure from anti-apartheid groups and black African archaeologists, South African archaeologists of all persuasions were excluded from the Congress. This move was opposed widely by champions of academic freedom, and many of these withdrew. This caused the biggest split that British archaeology has ever experienced, with permanent damage to personal and academic relationships (Ucko, 1988). Subsequent conferences of the congress have been notable for the incorporation of a wide spectrum of Third World participants, and the development of a *world* archaeology, rather than one largely centred on Europe and North America.

After this whirlwind and superficial tour of other countries' archaeology and politics, we may ask whether the motivation for British archaeology is equally various or dubious ethically, and this is the subject of our next chapter.

# 3

# British Archaeology

What of British archaeology? Is it all geared to academic research of a disinterested kind, free from all taint of political bias or other distortions of the truth for non-scholarly ends? Not quite, I fear. Among the motivations listed above we appear on the whole to be free of any attempt to give priority to nationalist interests. King Arthur is an interesting example. If he existed as a historical figure at all, it was as a champion of the Christian British (in the dark age following the end of Roman Britain), against the threat of incoming English (Anglo-Saxon) immigrants. But in the twelfth century we find him as a popular folk-hero of the British, by that time Welsh and English together. Today, at the popular level, Arthur has a major following, and gets as much press as the thoroughly English cake-burner Alfred, though the two are conflated in the popular mind, as in *1066 and All That*, where the paragraph on the famous cakes alternates Arthur and Alfred as the one responsible – here as a national hero opposing the Vikings.

Indigenous prehistory is accorded no more public or academic support than the archaeology of the wholly alien Romans, though Boudicca, the Iron Age queen who revolted against Roman rule, is another popular heroine. The British west of the 'Dark Ages' is studied with its early Anglo-Saxon (enemy) counterpart in the east. Anglo-Saxon Sutton Hoo (chapter 8) is a prestige project, but so too is Viking York. The castles and churches of invading Normans are the subject of extensive studies. On the other hand, one of the most costly recent operations, the lifting from the seabed of the wreck of Henry VIII's battleship, the *Mary Rose*, was undoubtedly helped by nationalist feeling that Britain was 'great' in those golden Tudor days.

Wales and Scotland do of course have nationalistic aspirations to self-government. In archaeology, this is reflected in the museums, in the sense that they display local material, such as that in the National Museum of Wales. In contrast to this mainly evenhanded interest in Britain's own past, some British archaeological resources are directed extensively to the past of *other* countries. Many academic archaeologists do field research in other countries, increasingly to the annoyance of their inhabitants. Even in Wales, the excavation hut of an English archaeologist was daubed 'English Go Home', but not burnt down.

Figure 3 shows the outline of a Roman fort in the university campus at Birmingham which was largely destroyed without excavation by the university's own buildings and car-parks, while its archaeologists were directing their research elsewhere. Such digging as was possible was done instead by the Birmingham Archaeological Society. This is a kind of inverse snobbery, the belief that somehow Britain is a bit peripheral, compared to the 'great civilizations' of Rome, Greece or the Near East. This view has been considerably modified in recent years by the advent of absolute dating, such as that from radiocarbon. This shows that some of our major prehistoric monuments, including megalithic tombs, are actually earlier than the eastern Mediterranean 'prototypes' from which they were supposedly derived by the process of 'invasion' or 'diffusion' – two explanations of culture change that have gone out of fashion in recent years.

TOURISM AND THE CULTURAL HERITAGE

Archaeology is used in England for public education, through tourism, centred on archaeological sites and monuments, national parks, 'heritage centres', 'theme parks' and museums. The 'cultural heritage syndrome' (Hewison, 1987; see also chapter 9)

*Figure 3* Metchley Roman fort, University of Birmingham

– the enlightenment of people about their past – is one of the chief planks on which archaeologists in this country try to get funds from central or local government. At Bordesley Abbey near Birmingham, our excavations provide an 'ancient monument' for the New Town of Redditch, giving new immigrants into the area some roots in a sense of history.

We have had, until recently, an excellent record in public education through our 'ancient monuments'. They have been well cared for and displayed, at considerable public expense. Gate receipts were low, except for such popular sites as Stonehenge (where the associated archaeological evidence was in danger of being worn away by visitors' feet). This was partly because the general public did not understand the monuments: a chunk of ruined masonry labelled 'reredorter' is not very evocative unless the tourist is versed in medieval monastic architecture and space-function.

There has accordingly been a trend in recent years not only to 'liven up' our monuments and make them more educational at a more popular level, but also to make money out of them by 'privatization'. The model here was the exploitation of 'historic houses' by their blue-blooded owners. There was a (fortunately erroneous) rumour that lions were to be introduced into Fountains Abbey, a magnificent Cistercian ruin in Yorkshire. The older framework concerned with ancient monuments was scrapped and a new, semi-autonomous Historic Buildings and Monuments Commission (English Heritage) was set up. Significantly its first chairmen was Lord Montagu of Beaulieu, one of those very aristocrats who had commercialized their ancestral homes in order to survive. The outcome may not be so grim for archaeology as some fear, but clearly tourism and financial profit must not gain at the expense of a purely academic or educational approach. The related problems of tourism and the private sector in the heritage industry are discussed further on pages 167–70.

### RELIGION

Further down towards the 'dubious' end of the motivation scale are the promotion of religious truths (in this case Christianity) and, even worse, the support of myth. The latter is such a big topic that it has been reserved for another chapter (chapter 7). The former is worth examining briefly by a few examples, because the 'aspersions' I cast here are by no means supported by general academic opinion. The 'bending' of archaeological 'truth' is no more than a matter of being 'generous to the evidence' (a splendid euphemism in this context).

There is in Britain between the fourth and eighth centuries AD an overlap between the pagan beliefs of the Romans and early Anglo-Saxons, and the gradual spread (with some severe setbacks) of Christianity. The latter was either a remnant from Romano-British times, or the result of Irish missions or of those from Rome represented by such figures as Augustine and Paulinus, and described well by Bede. The relevant archaeological sites of this period – temples, churches and cemeteries – not surprisingly generate much academic discussion about their interpretation, whether pagan or Christian, or a mixture of the two. It so happens that the archaeologists concerned (and indeed most of those who study undoubted *churches* and their surroundings) are themselves Christians. This has, perhaps understandably, caused them to lean towards a Christain interpretation of borderline cases which is not always fully warranted by the evidence. Two examples must here suffice.

Many graves in the later Roman period in Europe are orientated west–east (heads to west). These include many cemeteries which are undoubtedly non-Christian. This fashionable orientation was taken over by Christians (without any authority of Holy Writ) and is with us to this day, as is the similar orientation of churches. To infer, however, that a cemetery of west–east graves in (say) the sixth or seventh centuries is Christian, in the absence of an associated church, is quite unjustified, but is very common even in present-day academic archeological writing.

My second example is Tintagel. For a long time the ruins on this splendid Cornish headland were believed to be 'King Arthur's Castle'. Indeed they are still called this locally. Tintagel village is rich in 'Halls of Chivalry', 'King Arthur's car-park' etc. Although the largest ruins on the headland are indeed those of a castle (of medieval date, centuries later than Arthur), excavations in the 1930s and 1940s revealed a number of structures of a lesser order, and a great many finds. The finds are of the greatest interest. They include pieces of hundreds of pots which were made not in Cornwall, but in very far distant places in North Africa and the Eastern Mediterranean. There they can be dated firmly to the fifth–seventh centuries by coin evidence, and since the areas concerned were fully Christian by this time, some pieces exhibit as decoration Christian symbols – crosses, alpha/ omega, saints etc. The trade or other mechanism by which such pottery was imported into Britain is a matter of continuing debate.

One interpretation, favoured by the excavator of Tintagel and by others, is that the pots were associated with Christian movement directly from those areas into Western Britain and Ireland. They are parts of *amphorae* (general-purpose containers for wine, olive oil or foodstuffs) and tableware. The 'Christian' interpretation was that they were for use in the Mass, the tableware being for the Host, and the *amphorae* for the wine. The excavator interpreted the stuctures uncovered as those of a Celtic monastery, similar to early monastic sites in, for example, Egypt (Radford and Swanton, 1975). There is, however, no evidence that would be accepted by modern, 'rigorous' archaeologists that the pottery was associated with these structures at all. Current opinion is that the latter are medieval, and associated with the castle; and that the pottery rubbish is from secular buildings of considerable importance in areas not yet excavated. The pottery would in this case be 'prestige' material associated with an important chief, or with a major administrative, meeting or trade centre. Perhaps after all King Arthur was nearer the mark – the pottery is at least of a suitable date!

### THE JEWISH CEMETERY IN YORK AND OTHER SKELETONS IN THE CUPBOARD

Another interesting example, of quite a different kind, of the effect of religion on archaeology in Britain is provided by the excavation of the Jewish cemetery in York in 1983. York has a bad name, even today, with the Jewish community, similar to that of Belsen or Auschwitz. This is because of the massacre of Jews in the castle tower there in 1190 (all Jews were expelled from Britain exactly a hundred years later, in 1290). There is good historical evidence that the Jews of York and other towns nearby were buried in an area in York called Jewbury. Accordingly, when in 1982 the area was sold for development as a car-park associated with a new Sainsbury's supermarket, the York Archaeological Trust pointed out the historical evidence, and the possibility of a large Jewish cemetery being encountered. Support was sought for excavation from both Sainsbury's and from the Jewish community, in the belief that it was better for the cemetery to be carefully (and decently) excavated by archaeologists than to be churned up by bulldozers.

The Chief Rabbi in London (Lord Immanuel Jakobovits) refused even to countenance the idea of a Jewish cemetery being disturbed; he did, however, support a proposal for an excavation to see whether burials were, in fact, present, provided that no bones were moved. A trial excavation in the threatened area did indeed reveal many graves, orientated north–south. There were nailed wooden coffins, of men, women and children, and of medieval date. The Chief Rabbi was again approached, and the discoveries were considered by the Court of Beth Din. The Court refused to believe that the graves found were those of Jews, who, it was said, were never buried north–south or with coffin nails; and no Jewish objects or tombstones had been found. In fact, the only evidence for the cemetery being Jewish was that of 'very old documents'. In effect they washed their hands of the whole matter.

Since the existence of a cemetery (whether Jewish or not) had now been proved, Sainsbury's were under a legal obligation, under an English law of 1981 (Disused Burial Grounds Amendment Act), to remove all skeletons from areas to be disturbed. Under the Home Office licence issued to them they undertook to remove and rebury the remains 'without undue delay' in adjacent 'safe' ground. They contracted this work to the York Archaeological Trust (rather than to professional 'cemetery-clearing' firms which do, suprisingly, exist). In the spring and summer of 1983 over 500 graves were excavated, making this a cemetery of the greatest interest to students of medieval burial practice and of medieval human skeletons. No archaeological evidence was in fact found for the cemetery being Jewish (what could there be, in the absence of grave memorials?); but the coincidence of a large medieval cemetery with distinctive burial rites, not associated with any known church, and the historical evidence left very little room for doubt that it was the Jewish Cemetery of York that had indeed been excavated.

Work proceeded on the analysis of the results, on the measurement of the bones, and on the search for any evidence of disease (such as arthritis or leprosy) or accident. This was done by human biologists at the University of York, with the aid of research funding provided by the Science and Engineering Research Council. Interest generated a short account late in 1983 in the local newspaper, of 'Jews' skeletons being measured in York'; this was copied in *The Guardian*. Even though the Chief Rabbi disclaimed interest, a trainee rabbi and students of the orthodox Jewish College at Gateshead made a strong protest to him at the very concept of the measurement of Jewish skeletons being discussed in the public press – and in York of all places!

The Chief Rabbi may have had second thoughts about his earlier pronouncements, for he immediately complained to the Home Office. They, duly sensitive to the interests of religious minorities in Britain, ordered their representative in York, the local Environmental Health Officer, to order immediate reburial. Sainsbury's were asked to dig a hole for reburial and the university to give up the bones. Sainsbury's, the York Archaeological Trust and the University of York all have a public image to maintain, so could hardly provoke a major scandal by refusing. Representations were, however, made to the Chief Rabbi and the Home Office, to give more time to complete the scientific examination.

In the event, a week's reprieve was granted before the bones were removed to a Jewish mortuary, to await reburial months later, but the biological examination was by no means complete, and the record is accordingly deficient. Members of the Jewish community from Manchester came to collect the bones from the university, and others from Gateshead came to make sure the whole process was carried out with reverence. The former group in fact expressed great interest in the biologists' findings; they could appreciate that the archaeologists had recovered evidence relevant to the history of the Jewish faith that would otherwise have been destroyed by Sainsbury's bulldozers; they described the research as 'fascinating'.

Each skeleton was placed in a separate heat-sealed polythene bag, with a plastic identity disc. These were then put in wooden boxes. The Jews who collected these from the university hoped that it would be possible to re-inter them in the area of the new supermarket *in the same pattern as that in which they had been excavated*, using the archaeologists' plan of the cemetery to achieve this end. To have carried this out would have needed a plot of land as large as that which the cemetery had formerly occupied, which just was not available in the crowded urban area of York. While negotiations proceeded on this point between the Jewish community and Sainsbury's, the bones were stored in the Jewish mortuary at Manchester.

The Jewish community wanted 300 rabbis to be present at the ceremony of re-interment, but Sainsbury's did not think it was possible to accommodate more than a few in the rather restricted area available. The bones were finally reburied on the same day as lightning destroyed the roof of the south transept of York Minster, from which we may draw our own conclusions. There is now a plaque at the entrance to the supermarket car park, recording these events, which reads (in Hebrew script and English):

This is the location of the ancient Jewish cemetery of York. Some of the remains were re-interred 8th July 1984 – 8th Tammuz 9744, in the presence of the Chief Rabbi, Sir Immanuel Jakobovits, and representatives of the Jewish community. The re-interment site was kindly provided by J. Sainsbury PLC, to whom the Jewish community is most grateful. The ancient cemetery approximated to the present car park area.

This was not the first time that the Jews had objected to the disinterring of Jewish skeletons. A more serious case was that in Jerusalem in 1982, where there were near riots of protest against archaeologists excavating graves. This protest spread to Britain; a protest meeting was held in South Kensington by orthodox Jews protesting about the excavation of the ancient patriarchs; a photograph in *The Times* showed protestors at the meeting, holding up in their midst a skeleton (which we must presume was a plastic one used for medical teaching). Israeli law now lays down that no excavations may be made within half a mile of any known Jewish cemetery. Jewish objection to the excavation of graves by archaeologists is not, however, confined to those of Jews. A wider basis of protest, which is also shared by many non-Jewish people, is encapsulated in the following extract from a *Times* special article (11 January 1984) by Bernard Levin (himself a Jew), which illustrates also how what began as a local archaeological problem in York had escalated to one of national and indeed universal interest:

## IF THESE BONES LIE AT PEACE, CIVILIZATION CAN SURELY REST

There was strange and little-remarked story the other day.... It concerned bones – 50,000 was the figure mentioned.... The bones came from graves which were believed to be those of Jews; ... our century has seen Jewish bones produced in quantities never attained in all previous history, though ... the massacre of Jews at York in the twelfth century had more than a touch of the murderous frenzy that raged in civilized Europe less than 50 years ago. The Chief Rabbi asked the archaeologists to cease work on the examination of the bones and rebury them where they had been found. His reason was 'the paramount concern for the reverence due to mortal remains which once bore the incomparable hallmark of the divine image, and which, we believe have an inalienable right to stay undisturbed'. He added that 'dignity shown to human remains, even centuries after death, could contribute more than any scientific inquiry to human civilization.' ... Those bones may now sleep soundly, undisturbed by the trolleys of Sainsbury's customers, until they wake never to sleep again.

A final example of the potential disapproval of the disturbing of the dead by archaeologists refers to work at the medieval Cistercian Abbey of Bordesly, Redditch, near Birmingham. The source is the rather unexpected one of *Treasure Hunting* (November 1982), the magazine of the metal-detecting fraternity. They are here using *Roman Catholic* disapproval to back up their many-pronged attacks on establishment archaeology; this is the first time I have been described as a 'ghoul'.

## ARCHAEOLOGICAL 'GHOULS' UNDER CRITICISM

The disturbing of the dead by archaeologists is yet again under criticism. This time a team of forty archaeologists (led by Professor Philip Rahtz) are interfering with 150 graves – some of them belonging to Catholic monks – on a dig being undertaken in the ruins of Bordesley Abbey.

Former Redditch police sergeant Richard Thornton-Pitt, himself a Catholic, has spoken out in condemnation. 'They shouldn't be interfering with these holy men buried in consecrated ground, it simply isn't right', he commented. 'How would they like it if someone dug their parent up?' This is not the first occasion on which local Catholics have had to stop archaeological grave-robbing. In 1967 Father Bede Moore presided over the reburial of a skeleton excavated from the Abbey cemetery 800 years after the original burial. 'It was decided he should be properly buried again rather than just becoming a souvenir piece', Father Bede commented.

The problems encountered here are part of a world-wide concern about the disinterment and reburial of the dead, already referred to in the case of Australia (pages 33–6): concern sufficient to warrant a whole congress on the subject at South Dakota in 1989 (Hubert, 1988; Rahtz, 1988a).

51

### INDIVIDUALS AND INSTITUTIONS

Much archaeology in Britain is motivated by the desire for self-aggrandizement of individuals or institutions. Such motivation is, however, normally concealed by a more respectable umbrella – I claim that I am writing this book to invite readers to become interested in archaeology, to educate them to want to know more, to promote a greater understanding in the cultured world about the framework within which archaeology works. All these are true to some extent, because it is by doing such things that I achieve or maintain status in society (hopefully not the reverse!) and satisfy my own intellectual and expressive needs. Similarly, when the British Museum hangs on to the Elgin marbles, it does not honestly admit that it wants to maintain its high status (as the place where the Elgin marbles may be seen) but builds up a complex justification based on London being a more convenient place for world scholars to see the marbles, a sort of international museum. Similar attempts at survival in society determine most archaeological work in Britain, though heavily and on the whole successfully disguised.

### TREASURE-HUNTING

We need not dwell on the lowest of all motives for doing or promoting archaeology, that of treasure-hunting, profit or looting. In Britain as elsewhere, there has been digging for cash, or saleable or convertible objects, since at least Roman times, often with high approval. The findspots are not properly recorded, and the finds themselves do not always reach museums where they can be studied or published. The situation has vastly deteriorated in recent years because of the extensive use of metal detectors, and their high success rate. Most metal-detector users or clubs are merely ignorant of the evidence they destroy when they dig up a 'bleeped' find, but a hard core minority known only too well. They study archaeological publications to find out where to dig, and to find out what is valuable. They regard archaeologists as self-righteous spoilers of their pleasure and profit, when attempts are made by legislation or social pressure to restrict them. They are sometimes encouraged by land-owners or farmers in return for a 'cut', and it is even rumoured that some museums buy their finds, and advertise that they will. They justify this by saying that it is better for illicitly-acquired items to find their way to museums rather than to dealers.

One such firm of antiquity dealers, Fox and Company, of Yeovil, Somerset, advertises finds from all over the world. Many are from Britain, usually given a vague location, such as 'North West Wiltshire'; or more specifically, Lamyatt, a temple site which suffered severely at the hands of local depredations. Three lead 'curses' (incised inscriptions on lead sheets, asking the gods to punish someone who has done wrong to the writer) were found by metal detectors at the temple site of Pagans Hill, in Somerset, which I partly excavated in the 1950s. They were subsequently sold to Fox and Company, who fortunately allowed them to be examined by experts, but of course I have no idea in what part of the site they were found, or at what depth.

In fairness to metal-detectorists, it must be stressed that many are now helping archaeologists in their work in very constructive ways; and getting more satisfaction from their hobby in so doing. In searching for evidence of earlier settlements or cemeteries in areas which have been ploughed, they have, by finding all the metal objects, greatly increased the knowledge that can be gained from the finding of flints or bits of pottery. Moreover, the use of fertilizers has greatly accelerated the rate of decay of metal in the ground, so they are providing very useful data, notably coins, which would otherwise gradually vanish. The best results are when detectorists work directly with archaeologists on the same project or landscape study. Another good development is that even when detectorists work on their own, they are becoming more responsible. At a recent 'rally' near Dover, over four hundred converged on a large area of farmland for a weekend's detecting (with the full collaboration of the farmer); and they duly found a remarkable collection of antiquities, ranging in date from the Bronze Age to medieval, and including many finds from a hitherto unknown Anglo-Saxon cemetery. This sounds rather horrific, *but* they did use a very modern and expensive surveying instrument to record the exact position of each find.

All archaeologists like finding valuable or rare objects, and not only because they are very often also important evidence in the understanding of a site or period. This is only undesirable when their wish to find 'loot' determines the locality or strategy of excavation. Those who excavate and uncover many rich finds find it easier to get funds from museums for future work, in the expectation of further important finds accruing to the museum's collections. I was told by the editor of a county journal that their decision whether to publish my excavation report would be influenced by whether I deposited my finds in their county museum!

CONCLUSION

So Britain does have its non-academic reasons for the sponsoring or doing of archaeology. Each country has its own reasons for doing its own archaeology, dependent on its cultural and political history. Whatever the reasons, impeccably ethical or highly dubious, the work is done by archaeologists of varying integrity and quality. If all the archaeologists in the world were assembled together in a huge international conference, what would they have in common? What would distinguish this interesting gathering from one of economists, politicians or statisticians? What special qualities do archaeologists have to have? Are they born with a silver trowel in their hands, or do they acquire one by a cultural accident? There are questions now to be explored.

# 4

# Who are the Archaeologists?

In discussing the various factors which combine to give birth to, or make, an archaeologist, we must restrict ourselves to those who have 'succeeded' in the subject; those who are either in full-time employment in university, museum, field unit or public administration, or who are exceptionally talented amateurs. The last, although they earn a living by doing something quite un-related and futile like accountancy, are those who have made an important regional, national or international reputation by their work. Such a person is Leslie Grinsell who, while employed as a bank clerk, visited over 20,000 Bronze Age barrows in England, over a period of twenty years, and became the author-ity on them.

To be effective in archaeology, one has either to be a fairly low-level all-rounder like myself, who can do a reasonable job of excavating a site, publishing the results, doing some minor re-search, lecturing, travelling, writing or editing books, or training students; a brilliant theorist, who may never go near a dig; a synthesizer of other people's published work; or a specialist, such as someone who is the world's greatest authority on Roman wall-painting or Iron Age wheel-hubs.

It is always said there is a greater range among students with first-class degrees (bare firsts, good firsts, brilliant firsts, firsts of genius) than between them and the greater hosts of seconds and thirds. So too among archaeologists. The very top class are those who have an international reputation, and figure or will figure in any textbook on the history of the subject. These are the Darwins or Einsteins of archaeology. Such were General Pitt-Rivers, the founder of modern scientific archaeology; Gordon Childe, the European prehistoric theorist; and Mortimer Wheeler, perhaps the best-known archaeologist ever, familiar alike to academic and lay public through TV.

It may be invidious to single out exceptional archaeologists in our own day. Each country would have its own list. In Britain, in the 1990s, among the best-known archaeologists are Martin Biddle, who has directed remarkable excavations at Winchester, Repton, and St Albans; Barry Cunliffe, well known to radio and television audiences, and with a long list of famous excavations and books to his credit; Catherine Hills, an academic who also fronted the successful television series *The Blood of the British* and *Down to Earth*; Martin Carver, who succeeded me as professor at York, and directs the work at Sutton Hoo (chapter 8); and Peter Addyman, who has been responsible for the archaeology of York, mentioned several times in this book.

THE COMPLETE ARCHAEOLOGIST

Graham Clark (1965) defined the 'complete' archaeologist as follows:

The complete archaeologist, if such a being existed, would need to have a genius for travel, exploration, and reconnaissance; to be adept at business and administration, skilled at raising funds and obtaining all manner of permits from authorities and owners, few of whom can hope to gain from his activities, and capable of administering and directing excavations which may well turn out to be large-scale enterprises; to be a competent surveyor, draughtsman, and photographer, so that what he finds can be adequately recorded; to combine a gift for exact description and analysis with a power of synthesis and a flair for journalism; and to have the gift of tongues, or at very least an ability to digest the reports of his foreign colleagues without which his own will lack the authority that only wide reading and comparison can provide ...

– a formidable list of attributes for any one person to possess. Not all are needed to be a successful archaeologist, in particular a specialist. What *all* archaeologists need are, not necessarily in this order, an intense interest in the past, or in the theory of archaeology, bordering on the fanatical; a capacity for sustained hard work, often in far from ideal conditions either in the field, library or museum; high tolerance and acceptance of excruciating boredom; a lively but controlled sense of order, pattern, process and meaning; visual and conceptual imagination and a wide cultural perspective; and preferably, though it is not obligatory, an ability to communicate with other human beings in writing or speech. Since archaeology is about the whole past of human experience, it is especially useful to be a practical sort of person, knowing how things work, with some idea of how a farm is run, how a building is erected or how the dead are disposed of.

It is difficult to recognize the 'great' archaeologists of the next generation while they are students. Many of my most promising students have found jobs in archaeology; but others, equally good, have drifted into other professions, usually because they want to be in a well-paid job with secure career prospects. Archaeology offers neither of these.

To succeed in archaeology you have to *want to enough* (a very pregnant phrase); and you have to be *clever enough*; and you have to be in one way or another *lucky*. None of these is enough by itself. I do not know of any really good archaeologist who is not in a job in archaeology of some kind, however grim or poorly paid; but I know of many second-rate archaeologists in jobs who ought not to be employed at all.

How young does one have to start? Barry Cunliffe was interested enough to be doing field-work before he was 10; Stuart Piggott lectured to a Prehistoric Society field trip when he was 14 (but they didn't know that when they asked him!); Martin Biddle and Lawrence Barfield were directing an important dig together while they were still at school; George Boon published his report of a major Roman villa excavation before he was 21; and many other examples can be found of such prodigies, which are rather off-putting to the average aspiring undergraduate.

What we need to know about archaeologists, to find out what makes them tick, is their family, genetic and cultural backgrounds; who or what influenced them in school or university; what opportunities came their way in later years, and how and why they responded to them in the way they did. Such data would be interesting in themselves in our enquiry as to who is who and why, but also so that we may evaluate their published work in the light of all this. What biases are likely to be inherent in their approach (religious, Marxist, determinist etc.) which may have to be allowed for? It has been suggested that archaeologists should psychoanalyse themselves at intervals throughout their life, so that they can either minimize bias, or be explicit about it in presenting a 'loaded' view.

### THE ROADS TO SUCCESS

Many professional archaeologists enter the field by a conventional route: interest in archaeology at school, first degree in archaeology, doctoral thesis, experience in field, academic or other post. Barry Cunliffe went through this mill, after his precocious start; he was a lecturer in his early twenties, and was appointed professor of archaeology at Southampton at the age of 26. A surprising number of the 'top 100' in British archaeology did not follow this path. Several did not go to a university at all (such as Professor Stuart Piggott and myself); many did first degrees in law, history or science, and took up archaeology only as postgraduates. A few turned to it only in retirement. The most remarkable of these was Eric Higgs. He was a Shropshire sheep-farmer, with an amateur interest in palaeolithic archaeology. At the age of 56 he went to Cambridge as a student; later he was a research fellow and went on to be highly influential in early European prehistory; he initiated a new approach to archaeology based on a proper appreciation of the interaction of people with their environment.

## Who are the Archaeologists?

There are not enough detailed biographies or autobiographies of archaeologists. When they do get written, they are usually full of academic interest and often highly colourful, such as Wheeler's own autobiography, or the more personal biography of him written by Jacquetta Hawkes (1982), which treats of Wheeler's weakness for ladies as much as of his talents as an archaeologist. I would appeal to archaeologists who read this book to write their autobiographies in fearless detail. They should write a first volume at the age of 40, and add to it each decade thereafter, taking the opportunity to review and comment on what they had written earlier. These volumes would not necessarily be for publication (if they were honest, they would often be libellous or hurtful to the living) but as data for historians of archaeology in later times. Skinner, the early nineteenth-century antiquarian and archaeologist, wrote nearly a hundred such volumes. When he died by his own hand in 1840, he left them to the British Museum with instructions to open them only in 1900. They are now a major source for the social history and archaeology of his day, but one can see why he was reluctant for them to see the light of day while the objects of his acid remarks were still alive.

### ONE MAN'S STORY

I have written part of my autobiography, starting it, however, too late, when memory had faded (and worse, became selective). It is a difficult thing to be honest even with oneself; my experience has been that for an archaeologist at least, a thematic approach is likely to be more successful and useful than a chronological one, as long as there is some basic outline of events. While this is not the place for my autobiography, I end this chapter with a brief review of my career, including only those points that have a direct relevance to the themes of this book. It will serve as a case-study of why and how one archaeologist proceeded on his way.

I was born in 1921, the last of five children. My father had a double first in English and Science and became an authority on English grammar and a schoolmaster. As children we were taken

59

round on holidays to see castles, abbeys and museums, and doubtless this sowed some seeds. I did classics at school, and do remember being intellectually excited (a rare thing – school to me was purgatory) by J.E. Barton, the headmaster, lecturing with slides on Mycenae. After a barely passed Matriculation, I'd had enough of learning, and left school at 16 to be articled to a chartered accountant. I quickly realized the essential immorality of this profession (making the rich richer). From all this I was saved by the Second World War.

I had been interested in archaeology in a minor way since I was a caver on the Mendip Hills, in North Somerset, in my teens. I became aware not only of the Mendip landscape of barrows and other earthworks, but also of the archaeology that was associated in the area very much with caves and cavers. The latter, in the course of digging to get down into cave systems often found archaeological material (for instance, in Wookey Hole and the Cheddar Caves). Indeed the two interests were combined academically in the University of Bristol Spelaeological Society; this publishes both papers on scientific caving and on archaeology, in a journal to which I later contributed.

In the Royal Air Force I charged batteries, became an expert in the electrical side of radio-controlled bombs (the war ended just when we'd got the things working), but I also attended philosophy classes; and (perhaps most importantly for an archaeologist) learnt to put up with awful living conditions, and to 'get on' with the most unpleasant people I've ever met in my sheltered life. I ended up in 1944 as an education instructor, preparing airmen for return to civil life, teaching bookkeeping and current affairs. This was my start to a career in teaching and lecturing. More relevantly I was stationed on Salisbury Plain, near Stonehenge. Here I found myself in the next bed to Ernest Greenfield, a lifelong archaeologist who encouraged me, in our walks round the Plain, to develop my nascent interest in archaeology. My first archaeological 'lecture' was a 10-minute talk on the instructors' course, which was on the Mesolithic industries of Tardenois and the Mas d'Azil, culled from a popular text book.

After the war, in 1946, I began digging on my own in Somerset, helped by advice from Greenfield and local archaeologists.

This was not a job; I dug at weekends and holidays, helped by my wife and friends. I earned a precarious living as 'Studio Rahtz', a one-man business photographing babies, dogs and weddings. My first dig was what I thought was a Bronze Age barrow, but turned out to be a medieval windmill – perhaps prophetic of my later medieval interests. The second was a Roman temple at Pagans Hill, and this again had later Saxon and medieval finds. By 1950 I'd been accepted for an emergency training scheme for schoolteachers (which I nearly failed) and I taught in secondary modern schools in Bristol from 1951 to 1953. This was even worse than *being* at school, and brought out unsuspected latent homicidal tendencies. My only escape was to take the boys digging at Pagans Hill.

By 1953, I had established a local reputation in North Somerest as an amateur digger, and it so happened that in that area a new reservoir was to be built. Here was the element of luck. Brian O'Neil, the then Chief Inspector of Ancient Monuments, asked me to cut a section across a Roman road that was to be flooded; I agreed, very flattered. The big surprises were (a) I'd have a *hut* to put tools in, (b) I'd have *workmen* to do the digging, and – most gratifyingly – (c) I'd be *paid*. The job was to last two weeks, in the school holidays.

Construction work began that Easter, and huge machines churned up the landscape. In an area of over 800 ha where no finds had ever been made, sites turned up all over the place – prehistoric, Roman and medieval. The work had to be extended, Greenfield (then unemployed) joined me, and I burnt my boats. I resigned from teaching to become a professional digger for the Inspectorate of Ancient Monuments and anybody else who would pay me.

This was a risky thing to do; we were paid only by the day, and there was none of the security that teaching offered; I had moreover by that time three children. I was, however, more interested in digging than in attending to the welfare of my family. I dug full-time from 1953 to 1963, with some useful extramural teaching experience. I have excavated Mesolithic, Neolithic, Bronze Age, Iron Age, Roman, Dark Age, Saxon, medieval and post-medieval sites in fourteen different English counties (figure 4) and in Ghana, Yugoslavia, Spain and Greece. I have had a wealth of practical experience in many different soils and types of site – caves, buildings, Roman roads, cemeteries, villas, temples, watermills, churches, monasteries, palaces, moated sites, towns, castles, hillforts and even a Norman tunnel. More importantly, I learnt how to draw and write, and to *publish* the results of excavations.

By 1963, when I applied for a lecturer's post at Birmingham, I was able to cast quite a few excavation reports on the table, and got the job. I still had no degree, but soon after wrote an MA thesis on the Saxon and medieval palaces at Cheddar, which made me academically respectable.

It must be stressed that up to this point I had been merely a technician. I did the digs, and I described the results. There was little or no attempt to put them into a wider framework of research, or to *explain* them. With this I was at that time content, but now, in a university I was in a different ball-game. I not only had to teach students the *synthesis* of archaeology (principally medieval, since I was in a *history* department), but was expected to do real research rather than just digging things up, to make contributions to understanding rather than mere reportage. By 1968 I was having some success in synthesizing work on the Dark Ages in Somerset (Rahtz, 1982), with which my digs had been especially concerned. Since 1971 I have produced a steady output of papers on synthesis, and on theory and methodology, as well as more excavation reports. By 1991 I had published over a hundred reports or books, and a quantity of more ephemeral notes and book reviews.

In my academic career I had worked my way (or been pushed) up the academic ladder to Senior Lecturer and Reader, and was in 1978 appointed to the new Chair of Archaeology at York. In the light of my relatively non-academic background, this was a surprise (to me especially!), but also a challenge. I had by then formulated many of the ideas and attitudes expounded in this book, and I had also firm ideas on what should be learnt by archaeology and history undergraduates, and the methods by which they might most effectively be taught. York was the major challenge of my life.

*Figure 4*   P.A. Rahtz excavations, 1946–91

We designed a course that would enable students to learn *how* to do things (the practical side of surveying, digging, drawing, photography and writing); *what* the subject-matter of archaeology was – the basic data; and the *theory* that lay behind any attempts to use these data to improve understanding of the human past.

We concentrated largely on medieval archaeology (from the late Roman times onwards), a rather neglected period at that time. I gave my inaugural lecture on the application of modern archaeological theory (mostly developed in prehistory) to the medieval period. The subtitle of my lecture was 'King Arthur and his Random Number Table', which may give some idea of its flavour. More details of student and academic life at York are incorporated into the next chapter.

After my retirement, I became president of the Council for British Archaeology (CBA). I serve on various committees; act as consultant on archaeological matters; lecture on cruises; attend conferences; and travel widely for pleasure. All these activities keep me in touch with British and world archaeology, supplemented by the extra time I now have for reading. My wife and I also do some field-work, especially in Spain, where we now have a small house for winter use. But most of my time is given over to research, principally writing books, monographs and articles; especially I am concerned to publish all the excavations I have been responsible for, while I am yet able to write and draw. I still have a lot to write, but as I get older I hope to do a few other things that I've not had time to develop – understanding and playing music, and reading the classics.

This, then, is one man's story, the only one of which I can claim any knowledge. It has illustrated one rather uncertain path to becoming (eventually) an archaeologist, and it also serves as an introduction to what archaeologists *do* all the time, the theme of my next chapter. Archaeology is not, however, just *doing*, it is also *learning*. Archaeology has given me the education which I missed out on in my earlier life.

# 5

# What do Archaeologists Do?

There are many different kinds of archaeologist, and each spends his or her time in a different way. Some broad divisions are:

(1) Those who organize archaeology: they are really managers, the people behind the scenes, who provide the administrative framework within which other archaeologists work. Such are (in England) the inspectors of ancient monuments who do in fact actually 'inspect monuments', but mainly monitor the spending of public money; and the directors of big units, like York or London, who spend much of their time in public relations work, negotiating with developers, or fund-raising. Although they are trained archaeologists of high academic calibre (like Peter Addyman at York) they rarely dig themselves, but do edit the reports their staff write.

(2) The collectors of data: these are the main archaeological work-force. They include aerial photographers, regularly flying to locate new sites shown by changes in crop growth or parch marks over buried walls. These differences in the soil due to ancient activity can only be appreciated from some height. There are archaeologists who walk over every field or mountain in large areas, plotting on a map all finds of pottery, flint, bone and other material, so that some idea can be gained of the density of earlier occupation or land-use at different times. Others survey

every bump and hollow in the ground, and thus draw up plans
of prehistoric field systems or deserted medieval villages. Many
archaeologists are engaged in watching all disturbances in the
ground – by motorways, pipe-lines or quarrying – to record any
features or finds that may turn up. There are those who actually
do excavation, recovering complex data from the ground, or
working as divers below the sea. These are of course the ones
best known to the public, since they are always turning up something new – 'you never know what they may find'; this work
is considered more glamorous and exciting than walking over
fields, but it can be just as tedious.

In former times in Britain, and still in many countries, notably
the Mediterranean, the basic work-force consists of paid workmen, recruited for that purpose; they cannot be expected to take
much interest in what it all means, but can be extraordinarily
perceptive about strata and practical matters, because of their
wider experience in construction work or digging drains. Nowadays in Britain, the labour consists usually of professional
low-paid diggers (often archaeology graduates), students or
volunteers. Finally, some archaeologists work indoors, collecting historical data from documents and books, to enhance the
work of their colleagues in the field. Ethnographic 'collecting'
will be dealt with in the next chapter.

There is obviously some overlap between all these data-
collectors and our next group, the data-processors. Many people
will do both in the course of their work.

(3) The processors of data: aerial photographs have to be developed and printed, and plotted on to maps, before their usefulness can be realized; surveys of earthworks, or the results of field
finds plotting or destruction monitoring, have to be neatly
drawn up for publication. All finds recovered have to be cleaned,
marked, conserved, stabilized, identified and catalogued.

The afterwork in processing data collected in an excavation is
enormous, and the problem of doing so the principal reason for
the frightening delays between the excavation work and its publication. So much is involved on a complex site, so many specialists are brought in, that it can take twenty years or more to get

the data to publication. Even with my relatively good record of publishing my excavations, there are still one or two digs which I directed in the late 1960s or 1970s which are not yet published. This is not through any negligence on my part, but because of difficulty in getting specialist reports on bones, soil samples and so on.

It is also much easier to raise funds for excavations than for post-excavation work, even though four or five times as many hours have to be put into the latter as the former. In the Jewbury example quoted above (see chapter 3), Sainsbury's were legally bound to pay for the excavation – the 'removal of the skeletons' – but were not in any way committed to their study. Government grants given for the use of unemployed people in archaeological projects do not often extend to post-excavation work.

Specialist data-processors may work in museums or laboratories and are highly skilled, using sophisticated and expensive equipment. There is a machine set up at Oxford to do precise radiocarbon dating from samples of organic material such as charcoal, which cost half a million pounds.

(4) Analysers of data: again there is no hard and fast line between these and (3) or (2). Many of the data-processors are also engaged in the study of objects, in an effort to impart *meaning* to them in explanatory or historical terms. Some archaeologists will collect, process and analyse their own data, and might be hard put to say where one job began and another ended; there are nevertheless clear conceptual differences between (1) and (4), and there are many workers who will never get beyond (1), (2) or (3) to do (4) (such as technical draughtspersons). These are really technicians, who are providing the prepared basis for workers in (4) and beyond. Conversely there are those who are rarely engaged in (1)–(3) but who move in at stage (4), making 'sense' of masses of processed data. A number of archaeologists are currently employed as 'ghost-writers', preparing for publication reports of excavations which for various reasons cannot be written by the person responsible: the excavator is dead, has emigrated to Australia, has moved into a job which leaves no spare time, or is just incapable.

(5) The synthesizers: synthesis may be at site level, for instance in making overall sense of hundreds of graves in a cemetery; or at a local level, considering the settlement pattern in a particular parish (see, for example Wharram Percy in chapter 8); or at a regional level, such as the bringing together of all data on medieval villages in a county; or at a national level, for example considering all stone circles in Britain, or every Saxon shield; or even at the international level, comparing settlements in Germany with those in France, or megaliths in Malta with those in Ireland.

Parallel to these divisions of archaeology, we are also moving up the academic ladder, from the untrained workpersons to the pot-washer, from the site supervisors up to directors of excavations, up to the directors of units and the academic archaeologists in government institutions or universities. (1)–(5) are all really concerned with the *meat* of archaeology, the mass of processed and synthesized data that have accrued from many kinds of observations, and has hopefully been published.

(6) There yet remains the really important work, the *ultimate interpretation* of this material, to make meaningful statements about the past, either about *what* happened, *where* it happened, *how*, *when*, or more particularly, in the present climate of archaeological equiry, *why* it happened. *What* was it like to be an Iron Age smith? *Where* and *when* was iron-working first developed? *How* was it done in technical terms and, most importantly, *why* should anyone want to work iron in the first place? Why weren't people content to use stone or bronze any more? Flint tools had after all been around for thousands of years. Why was a need for change felt (if that is the explanation)? What were the economic and social factors which brought about such a revolution? And what changes resulted from such new developments in technology? Who masterminded the use of iron in any society?

By the time we have reached this level of archaeological work we are firmly in the academic world, in the universities or equivalent public or private institutions. Archaeologists working at this level are our 'leading lights' of the previous chapters.

From such 'big' questions and possible answers come even bigger problems of pure theory: what is the relationship of rubbish to human behaviour? What general laws of human behaviour may be deduced from our understanding of the past? What are humans essentially? And how do they differ from other species?

## WHAT IT'S LIKE TO BE AN ARCHAEOLOGIST

In the second part of this chapter we will be more realistic; we shall move from the above abstract classification of the hierarchy of work in archaeology, and examine what it is like to be in a particular job, or to be a student. We may not know much about the daily life of a Bronze Age farmer, but we *do* know about the daily life of a student, a worker on an excavation, a full-time professional working in a major unit, and a professor of archaeology. There are many other archaeologists' daily lives which could be described, but these are the four on which I can write with some knowledge. Inevitably, these pen-portraits are only partly generalized; they are particular representatives of a class or a place; the student is, for instance, a York student; the professional is in the York Archaeological Trust; the professor of archaeology is myself.

### The student

The student embarking on a degree in archaeology is usually a school-leaver. Some (and this is recommended) secure their university place and then take a year off, to travel or to get experience of 'life', and to get some digging experience, which few have acquired at school. There are also 'mature students' who have been working in archaeology at fairly low levels for some years, who have become very interested intellectually, and who now want to know more of 'what it all means'. A few of these are welcome – their commitment makes up for their usually poor school record.

The school-leaver has, generally, little idea of what archaeology means. Few study it at GCSE and A-level. Surprisingly few, when they come for interview, have even read a serious book on archaeology (as opposed to *Treasures of the Past* or *Did Space-men Build Stonehenge?*). It is possible to find out, by judicious discussion, whether they do have a genuine commitment, and are likely to be suitable 'blank pages' on which an understanding may be imprinted. Universities look for qualities of intelligence, imagination, a lively, outgoing personality and a wide range of cultural interests (including science-fiction!). If it appears that interviewees really are interested in *people* rather than *things*, they are advised to think again, and do history, anthropology or a social science.

Having surmounted the hurdles of getting a place, the student arrives and settles in. There is a difficult first term. There are often problems about adjusting to a mode of education where one has to *learn*, not to be *taught*, and to a life of freedom and tempting vices and pleasures. Students are often homesick or suffering withdrawal symptoms on the temporary or permanent cessation of an emotional relationship. In this difficult state, everything is thrown at them – the whole apparatus of living and working on a campus, and a welter of paper, syllabuses, reading lists and essay topics.

They are confronted by these strange people who live and breathe archaeology and who expect them to do the same. They soon find out that academics are actually human beings who, although they work hard, also play hard, and do ordinary things like gardening or watching TV.

Students at York settle down to a course on the city. They find out about the archaeology, architecture and history of the place where they are going to live for three years. Quite often it is the attraction of York as a famous historic city which has made them apply. They see York's digs, and meet the numerous archaeologists who work there in the field, in offices and in laboratories, and those who work in the archaeology of Yorkshire. There are lectures to be attended, both on York and on the principles and methods of archaeology, projects to work on, seminar papers to prepare and essays to write. It is all rather overwhelming, but by the end of term they at least know what archaeology is really about, have made new friends and are ready for a break in the bosom of a family Christmas (with a load of work and reading to do). In common with most university students, they develop very rapidly, so much so that their parents hardly know them; some blame the university for having brought about such changes in their dear daughter or son.

In the rest of the first year they go on a residential field trip to a distant area; they learn more about the principles of collecting and analysing archaeological data, and of the practical skills of surveying and field-walking. They learn how to talk, to expound rather than read seminar papers, and study a substantial topic such as 'the origins of urbanism'. They have learnt, with varying degrees of success, how to combine work with pleasure, how to skim books without actually *reading* them, and how to cope with incessant demands for more and better work. A group identity develops, and discussion begins to take off. The ideal seminar is one in which it wouldn't matter much if the lecturer left the room. Personal tensions have become resolved, or *modi vivendi* worked out. By the end of the year, it is clear to the students and to the staff who is working really hard and developing a wide understanding, and who is only doing the basic minimum to avoid getting hauled over the carpet or, in extreme cases, getting sent down. A few find in this first year that archaeology (or even university life) is not for them – they 'drop out'. The great majority do, however, cope very well with the demands of an archaeology course.

In the first summer vacation, the student does several weeks of excavation, usually on the sites that the department sponsors or runs. This experience provides a splendid change from indoor course work, a chance to get fit, and a very wide social experience. Working as a team, for seven or eight hours a day, six days a week, they really get to know each other, and enjoy collecting and analysing absolutely new data. One of the things which archaeology has especially to offer is this opportunity to be right at the working-face of primary research; students frequently make important discoveries and, more importantly, deduce their overall significance. They soon realize that it isn't just the 'experts', the professionals, who find out all the interesting things in archaeology; it can be *them*. Most do very well in the field. There are inevitably a few Jonahs and moaners ('it's wet, it's cold, the food is awful, I've hurt my back, I've got a blister, can't we go to the pub? Yerghh, I've cut a worm in half'), and one has to admit that there are students who will do better at 'book' archaeology, and should avoid trowels, mud and wheelbarrows. This doesn't matter; archaeology needs all kinds of talent, intellectual ones especially; but it's important that all synthesizers, all *users* of archaeological data, should know how they are obtained, with what blood, sweat and tears, and how reliable the published account is likely to be. (See 'How likely is likely?', reprinted here in chapter 7.)

The summer is formative: this is when some students really get bitten by the bug, and decide that they will become archaeologists by hook or by crook. Commitment to the subject is usually intensified, and when they return to the university in the autumn it is with an air of purpose. Further themes are studied (churches, monasteries, technology, urbanism, burial practices) and further skills acquired (drawing, computing, photography, laboratory work). They also begin work on their own piece of research – a dissertation, in which they develop skills of bringing data together into a form suitable for publication. Some of these dissertations are of a remarkably high standard, and some do eventually get published, an invaluable step in a professional career.

Assessment looms large in student minds. Although entrenched in university structure in Britain, and in the expectations of contemporary society, it is not what education should be about. But we have to grade and to rank, and the competitive element does, in our socially undeveloped society, act as a spur to hard work. An eye to the material rewards of 'doing well' is a powerful incentive, however distasteful this may seem to those of us who see universities as places to foster intellectual development. Assessment is by a number of examiners, including one from another university, and is based on a broad spectrum of effort: dissertation, lecture, seminar, portfolio, field-work and written examinations. When all this is finished, there is the grand ceremony of degree day; everyone wears academic finery, and proud parents see their offspring hooded and gowned, receiving BA degrees at the hands of the chancellor.

Graduates who are outstanding may go on to do research for a higher degree, but these are increasingly rare, not because of shortage of talent but because (in the 1990s) of financial restrictions imposed by an economically orientated central government in Britain.

The rest try to get jobs, short-term or long-term. Any experience here is valuable, however lowly it may seem at the time. The important thing is to survive, and preferably by doing archaeology. Some decide to opt out and seek more lucrative offers in the civil service, merchant banking or industrial management.

One skill that is being learnt is how to work in archaeology while surviving on social security. Increasing unemployment may well make this more acceptable in our society; and monetary benefits may be more readily available in future to those who are working at something worthwhile.

Even if students don't become full-time 'professionals' or 'gainfully unemployed', archaeology will remain an important part of their lives, to be worked at as and when opportunity offers, notably in early retirement.

### The worker on an excavation

Here we can do no more than delineate what one would see if one visited an excavation and saw people at work. I describe here the scene at Wharram Percy, as it was in 1990. This should be read in association with the wider aspects of that site, dealt with as a case-study in chapter 8 (see also pages 83–6 below, on tools and techniques).

On a big excavation like this, where over a hundred people are sometimes involved, there is a considerable infrastructure. The work is done mainly on a rota system, with only one professional (the cook). So we see people preparing vegetables, washing up and emptying latrines. Some faithful volunteers maintain the hot showers, repair tools and surveying equipment, make benches and cut up wood for the fire. If we eavesdropped on the morning briefing after breakfast, we'd hear the jobs being assigned and the comments on shortcomings of those who left the gates open, or left their late night 'coffocoa' mug unwashed. There would be a weather forecast (wet, cold and windy), a report on the state of a 'lurgi' affecting diggers (a bug that lives at Wharram and comes out each year to give people stomach upsets – in Spain it's there all the time!), and any interesting news, such as war breaking out in a far-away real world, or important visitors expected; lectures, walks, excursions and films being organized.

By 9.15 a.m. everyone is at work. The major activity to be seen now is digging. The workers are also finding things, such as bones, pot, stone tools or charcoal. These are being put into bags or containers marked to indicate precisely where they were found. Plastic labels in waterproof ink are being written to affix to the ground. Every different area of soil, every hole, every wall, every patch of stones, in fact every *context* has its own number and description; these may run into hundreds or thousands on the average excavation.

The site supervisor sees to all this, overseeing the work of other people. Periodically there is a need to straighten up and stretch (trowelling induces muscle cramp) and make notes. There must not be too much noise (no idle chatter or radios, please); all that should be heard is the gentle clink of trowels on stones, the swush-swush of brushes, measurements being called out, an earnest discussion on interpretation, the munching of cows, and the high noise of larks.

Other workers are using survey instruments, drawing patterns of stones and sections of soil, and measuring the position of finds. Periodically, photographs are taken. The finds and drawings are taken to nearby huts, tents or caravans. Drawings are inked in and neat copies made, context sheets are checked, and the finds go to a special finds department, run by a finds supervisor, who will organize their cleaning and marking. The finds are then 'viewed' by site supervisor and director, to assess their date and singificance, classified, catalogued, and bagged or boxed. There may well be specialists at this stage – on this site there is a caravan specially set up for classifying and drawing pottery (the latter after bits have been stuck together), and for identifying animal bones.

An important figure is the photographer. All parts of the site are visited at regular intervals in a Land Rover loaded with cameras. Photographs are taken in monochrome and colour, slides and prints, using a high tripod, the Land Rover roof or a high photographic tower. A record is kept of each take, and these are recorded in an index and noted in the excavation records.

The director of the excavation has done a lot before the excavation starts, deciding where and how to dig, organizing the transport of the equipment to the site, laying out the space around the dig, organizing money, stationery and consumables, and generally seeing that all systems are 'go' by the time most of the work-force arrives. It is then important to see that all goes well, to encourage people, to deliver rockets if something has gone wrong, to check recording, discuss interpretation, assess finds and generally try to keep track of everything that is happening. A special notebook will be devoted to any general points of interpretation and the director may be seen walking round the site periodically, talking into a tape-recorder. Some have recently begun to talk to a video-camera while filming. The director also has to keep up morale and quell mutinies, usually in appalling weather. A bottle of whisky can be sent round for communal swigging (the bottle is an object often to be found in the backfill of archaeologists' trenches); or the whole job may be stopped, everyone piled into the Land Rover and taken to the nearest pub.

The director also digs, either (as in my case) because he or she likes shifting dirt from one place to another, or to be closely involved in crucial areas where there is a need to *see* exactly what relationships are being revealed, and to make sure their significance is fully appreciated and recorded.

The workers, and especially the supervisors, should be kept in touch with all that is being done and discussed, new data that have been found or new theories propounded. This is absolutely crucial if everyone is to work meaningfully, and is usually done after tea. An uninformed digger is a bad and unhappy one.

The responsibility for writing up the site for publication rests

75

on the director; the better the records have been kept, the easier this will be. Workers rarely learn how to record properly *until* they have had to write up an excavation (which is difficult to arrange!). Increasingly it is good to involve many people in post-excavation to underline the necessity of good recording.

Finally the dig is finished, and all data have been extracted from the ground. This is when most of the work-force remember pressing engagements elsewhere, leaving a few heroic figures (including the director) to the back-breaking task of dismantling, cleaning and transporting the equipment, vehicles and stores. The director can usually rely on some faithful helpers to stay on (usually arranged beforehand) for a day or two, to pack everything away.

So much for the excavation itself. There are often other things going on, which although not digging, or providing the infrastructure, are part of the project as a whole. We may see people making a record of plants and flowers now growing in the environment (were they always there?), catching small mammals in boxes at night: they like this, it's warm, and the same ones come back the next night. Others will be recording the gravestones or measuring the church and drawing it stone by stone; 'laying out' excavated buildings for visitor displays; showing visitors around (a good exercise for the diggers), and finally going round local fields and farms, recording finds in the ploughsoil, assessing modes of current land-exploitation and management, and recording old people's memories of former times.

This account of what it's like to work on an excavation probably gives a rosy view, based as it is on a research dig taking place in an isolated rural landscape. This is very different from working in a town, as my next section shows.

## The professional in a unit

The world of the big urban unit, like the York Archaeological Trust, is altogether more professional than most other excavations. This is not to say that the archaeology is better, or the staff more committed, but there is obviously a very different atmosphere on digs that go on for several months compared with those that last only a few weeks. It is difficult to keep up enthusiasm in these circumstances, especially when the digging goes on throughout the winter in very unpleasant conditions of mud and cold. Only the toughest professionals can take this sort of thing and at the same time keep up efficient recording. A very tight team spirit develops in these circumstances, and a certain *machismo*.

The urban unit exists to deal with the archaeology of an important historic town, notably with the threats that arise from development and renewal. At York there has to be close collaboration with the City Council, the planning authority, to find out what development is approved in this year, next year or some time in the near future. Once the scale and nature of development are known, the firm or contractor is contacted and informed of the archaeological potential of the area to be destroyed. Very often the developers are interested, for the sake of their public image, if nothing else, and give extensive support in cash or in kind, as Lloyds Bank and the General Accident Insurance Company have done in York.

City digs are complex. In York there are nineteen centuries of archaeology, and deposits can be seven or eight metres deep. They are immensely rich in structures and finds, and the conditions of preservation allow a great deal of organic evidence to survive: structures and objects of wood, leather, textile; mosses, beetles, plants and seeds; micro-organisms such as stomach parasites (York's cesspits provide a rich haul for the environmental scientist); and metal objects in pristine condition. Occasionally the finds are extremely valuable as well as historically important; one such was the discovery in a pit in York of a helmet of the eighth century, now insured for half a million pounds.

Not all threats can be coped with. There have to be discussions on priorities: what must be dealt with by a big and expensive excavation, what need only be trenched, and what can be largely written off with no more than observance of the destruction. A dig in the first category was Coppergate, which explored some of the richest Viking levels in Europe.

The staff of the Trust number nearly a hundred. There are

usually several excavation teams active at any one time, each with its supervisor and site finds department. At the Trust's headquarters there are draughtspersons, conservators, pottery specialists, photographers, find researchers and environmental scientists. It is estimated that a cubic metre of Coppergate's deposits contains half a million 'items' of scientific interest, many of which can be seen only under a powerful microscope.

There are people writing reports for publication in York's special series, and others editing them. There is of course an office staff to keep all this going – typing the reports, feeding data into a computer, paying salaries and maintaining co-ordination throughout the organization.

All this is the archaeology of York as planned research. There is also, however, in this case a quite separate organization, Cultural Resource Management Limited, whose staff handle all publicity, fund-raising, and the making and selling of souvenirs, replicas, Eric Blood-Axe mugs and T-shirts, postcards and slides. There are special shops in York where such things are sold, and a mail-order branch. CRM makes profits of many thousands of pounds, which help to keep the archaeological research going. This is likely to be increasingly important in the future, as central government gives less and less money, and looks with more favour on such schemes of 'privatization'.

At the head of this efficient organization is the director, Peter Addyman, a former university lecturer who chose to be at the sharp and professional end of archaeology rather than in the sheltered life of academia and students. He and his senior staff keep tight control over all the diverse activities of the Trust; they see that the publications come out regularly and are of high quality; they also disseminate the results to the archaeological world by lecturing to conferences and universities in Britain and abroad, notably in Scandinavia and the USA. Peter keeps himself cognizant with all that goes on, but has to spend much of his time on non-research activities, sitting on committees, giving lecture tours and securing royal and noble patronage. Queen Margarethe of Denmark is an invaluable partron, and takes an informed, academic interest in the work. Prince Charles, who read archaeology at Cambridge, has also been active in securing support.

The Trust takes its educational role very seriously. Its most ambitious venture is a major new museum, built on the Copper-gate site, the Jorvik Viking Centre, which now attracts half-a-million visitors a year. This is no ordinary museum of objects in glass cases and explanatory labels. After paying admission, the visitors sit in a small electric 'time-capsule' car. They are then taken on a time-travel tour backwards through the last ten cen-turies, emerging into a reconstruction of Viking Coppergate. The car moves slowly through a Viking street, where there are houses, rubbish, cats, excrement, and people quarrelling, trading and making things. All the appropriate noises are flung at the visitor in sixty-four-speaker ambient sound; the sound of people nattering and chattering in a market was recorded by Icelanders in Reykjavik. There are smells of fish, cooking, tanning, wood-smoke and dung assailing the nostrils. The time-cars approach the river where a Viking ship is moored, unloading its goods.

The cars then turn a corner and enter a replica of the archaeological excavation, where the time-travellers return to the present day, and see the evidence for all that has been experi-enced with all their senses in the first part of the trip. Finally the visitors come out into a splendid artefact hall, a spectacular display of finds, and a shop.

This imaginative and educational project is a worthy climax to many years of digging in York, and does a great deal to interest the general public in what archaeology really means, in a way that can be fully understood by everybody. The York Archaeological Trust has now paid off all the costs of the Jorvik Viking Centre (JVC) and enjoys an income of a million pounds a year from it. This is being used to fund the archaeological work of the Trust, and for further public education.

An even more remarkable recent enterprise in York paid for in this way is the Archaeological Resource Centre (ARC). Here the public can extend their experience of archaeology in ways very different from those available in most museums. People can handle a wide variety of finds rather than just look at them. They

79

are given a tray of finds which have been sieved, washed clean and dried; they can sort these into different categories: potsherds, animal bone, shells, glass, coins, plaster, slag, burnt clay and stone; there are helpers at hand to assist in identification. At a finer level, using a binocular microscope, very small finds can be discerned: pips, beetle-wings, excrement, fish-bones, seeds and pollen. Crafts can be practised, including spinning, weaving and making Roman open-work sandals out of prepared cut-outs and leather thongs. There are technological puzzles: how to use a medieval key and how to pick a Roman lock. Another popular attraction is interactive video, which displays typical archaeological data: finds, drawings, photographs and descriptions. From these the user is led through the process of post-excavation analysis: questions can be asked of the computer-based material, and users can arrive at the kinds of answers the archaeologists may give in their final publication.

All these experiences are to do with inanimate material; and as the director, Andrew Jones, points out, the real treasures of research are the living archaeologists; and these too can be seen. In an upper floor are glass-sided offices where the staff of the Trust are working in full view, analysing and treating finds; they cannot, however, be touched or talked to. The band of helpers downstairs is there to answer any questions about the work. The ARC is an entertaining and educational experience for everyone, from children to pensioners. This spin-off from a good tourist-orientated enterprise, the Jorvik Viking Centre, has thus led to public education in archaeology at its best.

## The professor of archaeology

Professors write books, among other things; the earlier drafts of this book were written sitting on a balcony of a room in a hotel in southern Spain, basking in hot sunshine. Occasionally I left my writing to go down for a swim in the sea across the road, or more warmly in the heated swimming pool below my balcony. In the afternoon my wife and I walked into the hills behind the hotel to do some ethnoarchaeology, a subject which will figure in my next chapter.

This is all very pleasant, but what else do professors of archaeology do?

The day is spent roughly equally between administration, teaching and research. Every professor has a role in running the university, sitting on committees, being part of the governing hierarchy under the leadership of the vice-chancellor. There is also much administration within the department. Although separate physically at York, the archaeology department is part of the university, with very close links with the central governing body. The administration handles all the paperwork concerned with admissions, fees and accommodation, and provides the entire financial framework within which the department operates. Archaeology departments are relatively small, compared with the 'giants' of physics, chemistry, biology or English.

Much time is taken up with answering letters. These vary enormously; there are requests for information on courses, enquiries about excavations past and current, and letters from cranks who have found a Roman villa or a stone circle in their garden, or have worked out King Arthur's pedigree. There are invitations to give lectures to conferences or local archaeological societies, and seminars to other departments of archaeology; to write books or take part in a TV programme. There are requests for references for past students, and letters from them seeking advice. There are funds to be accounted for, and problems about insurance, fire precautions, building maintenance and heating.

Teaching takes up a lot of time. In a small department the professor has to pull his or her weight, as well as making his or her own influence felt on students. In an average week in term time, ten hours a week may be spent in direct teaching – lecturing and tutoring – and many more in preparing lectures, chairing seminars, setting and marking essays, sorting out students' academic and personal problems, and just talking to them about their work or life in general. In the winter prospective students are interviewed, and in the summer there is the lengthy process of setting and marking examinations, having examiners' meetings, and deciding on and awarding degrees.

Apart from teaching undergraduates, there is the more demanding postgraduate teaching and supervision. Finally, in the summer vacation, a full eight weeks is totally taken up with excavations. The number of student contact hours here is probably more than in the whole of the rest of the year together.

University lecturers are, strange though it may seem, not appointed because they can administer or teach; no evidence of being able to do either of these things is asked for when one applies for a job. Nor is any formal training given to those who have no experience whatever of either (though this is changing). The sole criterion is research, whether the candidate is a scholar of some reputation a special field, as witnessed especially by his or her list of publications, and by the external referee's remarks. It is on the corporate research of its staff that the university bases its reputation. On appointment, one is expected to continue to publish and keep in the forefront of one's subject. Students obviously benefit from all this; teaching in a university may not be as efficient as it might be, but should be at the highest possible level in terms of giving a student a scholarly and up-to-date view of work in a particular topic.

Once appointed, the professor is expected not only to continue to be a leading light in the field, but also to act as leader for the staff. Normally they will already have special areas of interest, but the professor should be able to encourage and advise them, and try to organize the work of the department so that they can pursue research effectively, and incorporate it in the teaching. In this way the students feel they are part of a research institution and will be proud to belong to it.

Research is done principally in the evenings, weekends and vacations, as in term time the administration and teaching take up most of the time. But there *are* 168 hours in a week, and one has to learn to make the most of them and of the vacations.

A lot of research time is spent in writing up the results of excavations to the stage of publication. This involves basic ordering of the data, and putting the results into a wider structure of knowledge.

Some more general research may arise these reports. For instance, as a result of writing up a big Dark Age cemetery in Somerset, I got interested in why people orientate graves to different points of the compass. I gathered together all the data I could on the subject, and a publication called 'Grave Orientation' was the result. This treated the subject not within the narrow confines of Dark Age Somerset, but in different parts of the world through time. When I excavated an Anglo-Saxon water-mill at Tamworth, I knew nothing about such things, but I soon found out, and have since taken this on as a major research topic.

Much time is also spent on reading books on archaeology, keeping abreast of at least the areas taught, though even this is increasingly difficult with the enormous amount now being written. A great deal of the outdoor life of a professor is spent not only in excavating, but in travel, a form of open-air research especially appropriate for archaeologists, and involving far less organization than excavation. This form of travel with a research purpose is called ethnoarchaeology, and is the subject of my next chapter.

The life of a professor of archaeology is, then, a full one; full of hard work, challenge and stimulation.

When, the reader may ask, do I *live*? Well, to me, archaeology *is* life, and other things (and people) tend to get ruthlessly pushed aside for it. Fortunately my children are now all grown up with their own families, and my wife (she also works in archaeology as a freelancer) and I are free to do a good deal with out 168-hour weeks. We *do* do other things; when I get tired, I *stop*, and watch *MASH* or *Blackadder*. We read novels at bedtime and do a lot of exercise to keep fit, and we listen to music continuously when we are working. Unlike many people I cannot work in silence – I need a wall of music to shut me in with my thoughts or my drawing. So, on the whole it's a good life: digging, travelling, drawing, writing and *talking*.

TOOLS AND TECHNIQUES: EXCAVATION AND ANALYSIS

Archaeological excavation is a complex team operation. How it is done will depend on the aims of the work, the resources available (of people, money and time), the kind of subsoil and the type of site. In large-scale rescue digging, large machines may be used to strip off the upper layers. At Dorestad, in

Holland, most of a town of the eighth-ninth centuries AD was
stripped, covering many hectares; units of excavation here were
40 × 20 m (800 square metres) and each took only a few days
with twenty to thirty workers. At the other extreme, the excavation of a single grave with many finds may take one person a
week or more. At Wharram Percy (chapter 8) a careful hand-
excavation of 400 square metres took five seasons of three weeks
with an average of a dozen workers.

Apart from powered machines, the ordinary tools of spade,
fork, hoe, pick and shovel are in common use for the heavy
work, where a lot of soil has to be shifted. If a three-metre deep
ditch is to be emptied of the dirt which has filled it over the
centuries, careful use of smaller tools would make little impression. The standard tool for more careful work is, however, the
small mason's pointing trowel with a diamond-shaped blade; on
a dig everyone will have his or her own trowel in hand or in
back pocket. In dry conditions this is used with a hand brush,
with a hand shovel and small bucket to carry away the dirt to a
wheelbarrow or dumper truck, or on to a heap.

The area to be dug may be as small as one metre square (test-
holes to sample a large area), or trenches one or two metres
wide (for instance, to cut a section through a Roman road).
Most modern excavation is, however, done in areas ranging
from 10 × 10 m units upwards. Depths can range from no more
than 20–30 cm in open rural areas to the 6–8 m encountered in
deep urban deposits such as those of York or London, where
town-dwelling has caused the accumulation of millions of tonnes
of dirt and building debris.

The principle of excavation is to peel off accumulated layers of
dirt one at a time, beginning with the turf and topsoil, until all
humanly derived material has been removed, and natural, undisturbed subsoil or rock is exposed over the site. On the way
down, many features will be encountered, such as ditches, post-
holes, wall foundations, pits and graves. These are found by
noting differences in soil colour or composition, shapes or patterns which indicate to the experienced eye where there has been
an ancient structure or disturbance. To see these things, the work
has to be done very neatly, with no loose dirt or mess, and with

clean, straight edges. Each layer or feature has to be separately defined, numbered and removed, a careful record being made in drawings, photographs and words of its appearance, composition and extent. The position of any finds – pottery, metal, glass, stone etc. – is also recorded.

Excavation is destruction; normally at the end of the dig nothing remains except the natural rock, clay or gravel, with the shapes of holes cut in it by the features, such as ditches, whose fills have been removed. The only exceptions are where walls or floors are encountered, which will be preserved for people to see. Many visitors to digs are disappointed to find that what they are looking at and having explained to them will be removed or filled in again. The sad fact is that if anything like a wall or a floor, or even the post-holes of a palace hall are left open, they will very quickly deteriorate from weather, animals or vandalism unless a lot of money is spent in conservation and aftercare.

The dig finished, the site is filled in by machine or by hand, and the work of analysing the results begins. Many digs never get published at all, and the work in the field is seen as unjustified destruction of the evidence without record. In all these cases, it would have been better if the dig had never been done at all.

The post-excavation work is indeed complex, and demands skills which are more rare than those needed in excavation. Finds have to be conserved, drawn and reported on by specialists. A report on a big cemetery such as Jewbury, for example (see chapter 3), will involve human biologists for months or years in examining and measuring the human skeletons, to find out about public health, life expectancy, diseases and the make-up of the buried population. The written or computerized records and especially the drawings have to be collated, analysed and made sense of. Whereas in the excavation work proceeds from the latest levels to the most ancient, say from modern through medieval to the lowest Roman levels, in post-excavation analysis the process is reversed. The sequence of occupation is reconstructed in phases, beginning with the earliest and ending with the modern.

Text, drawings and photographs are finally assembled for publication. They go through the usual process of computerized or other typesetting, proofs and binding. Word-processors and automated typesetting play an increasingly important part. A lot of detail doesn't get printed, but goes into microfiche. This is a sheet of film with miniaturized transparencies which can be examined by the use of a special reader or magnifier; on a single small piece of film, there can be displayed ninety-six pages of text or drawing. A copy of this is put into an envelope at the back of the book. A more advanced technology is represented by the videodisk; this enables the student to have access to a much wider range of data, including moving images, such as those generated by computer.

Modern archaeological reports, unlike (I hope) this book, are difficult for the non-archaeologist to understand, increasingly technical, scientific and complex. Yet they are the fundamental record of what was found (and destroyed), and form the basis of all current and future research. Just as the modern dig recovers more evidence than those of twenty, fifty or a hundred years ago, so the amount of detail published increases in proportion. In a trial excavation on two Roman villas at Wharram Percy, a total of 50 square metres was dug in small holes or trenches. About fifteen people worked in the field on this for four days. The resultant report took five years to get together, and is a monograph of about a hundred pages with thirty-seven figures, with a further hundred plus pages in microfiche (Rahtz et al., 1986).

It is a pleasant moment for the director of an excavation when the printed copies of the report arrive, to be distributed to friends and colleagues. This is the end-product of a long process which began with the pregnant decision, 'let's have an excavation here.'

# 6

# Ethnoarchaeology, or How to Avoid Boring Holidays

Ever since Europeans moved out of their environment, and explored distant areas of the world where white people were an unfamiliar sight, they have evinced great interest in encountering peoples and societies whose lifestyle, economy and beliefs were fundamentally different from their own. To the Europeans of the sixteenth century, such peoples appeared to be 'primitive' and 'backward', ignorant of such basic things as the necessity to be decently dressed, the use of money, the smelting of metals or the existence of wheels and machines. Since Europeans of the sixteenth century and later believed themselves to be very admirable creatures, it was only a short step to regarding people of other cultures as 'inferior', suitable for extermination or exploitation in the interests of European prosperity.

A further, more interesting stage was to think that perhaps in these peoples Europeans could see a living representation of what our society had been like in prehistoric times. Hunter-gatherers in Africa, Australia or the New World could possibly provide analogues for our own pre-farming life. Flint, stone and bone tools found in prehistoric European contexts were compared with those still in use in areas remote from Europe, and their function thereby 'explained'. If, for example, a particular form of bone tool found in prehistoric Europe, whose function could not be guessed at, was exactly like one still used by Eskimos for skinning a seal, then it was assumed that was what our ancient tool was also used for. This was perhaps rather a naive way of reasoning, but it did begin the vast subject of cross-cultural correlation, in all parts of the world, and at all times, which has been such an important element in the development of modern world archaeology.

In the nineteenth and twentieth centuries, remote peoples at different cultural and technical levels have been a happy hunting ground for anthropologists. The latter increasingly became interested, not so much in seeking analogies for tools, but in the whole systems by which those people lived: their marriage, property and inheritance customs; ranking in society, religious beliefs and art; stages of life from infancy through puberty and adolescence to maturity and old age. These have become the classic agenda of social anthropology, the field study being known as ethnography (physical anthropology is concerned with racial types and human biology).

For a long time anthropologists studying remote peoples as ethnographers did so from a superior stance, rather as if the people being studied were some kind of super-monkey. Hand-in-hand with missionaries, soldiers and traders, they were the agents of oppression and had little real respect for other peoples' cultures, or for the idea that there might be alternative ways of living, rather than inferior ones. On the other hand, the idea of the 'noble savage', the purer and less corrupt life of the primitive, also influenced even nineteenth-century anthropologists.

### ETHNOGRAPHY TODAY

Things have changed. With the decline in a general belief in the ethics of colonialism and an increasing scepticism about the quality of life in the modern industrialized world (or even its chances of survival), there is a much greater respect (and even in some cases a sort of 'Garden of Eden' envy) for the lifestyles of Kalahari Bushmen, Alaskan Eskimos or Australian Aborigines. The last are regarded nowadays as one of the most successful races in having achieved a stable balance with the environment for 40,000 years. Ethnographers now approach their 'subjects' with something like humility, even though the last thing these peoples want to do is stay 'primitive' – they too want radios, TVs, motorcars and towns. In Ghana in 1966 I paid labourers 7s. 6d. a day (37.5 modern English pence) to work on my excavation. They did not need the money for the necessities of life, for those were provided by their community. What they saved up their wages for were transistor radios and football boots.

Although social anthropology has, through ethnography, built up a colossal world database for its subject, it has in recent decades been little interested in material culture or, rather surprisingly, in the *origins* of things and in their dynamics through time. Ethnographers are interested in *living* peoples, what they are doing *right now*. There is astonishingly little common ground with archaeology, even at Cambridge, where students study both subjects as part of the same degree.

## WHAT IS ETHNOARCHAEOLOGY?

Archaeologists interested in the material culture of other societies have had to do their own ethnography, and they called it ethnoarchaeology. It was not, for instance, until 1972 that the technical and economic base of aboriginal society in Australia was studied by archaeologists, and by then it was almost too late.

Ethnoarchaeology is the study of the *material culture* of *living* societies, which now include not only hunter-gatherers or farmers living in Africa, South America, the Arctic, Australia or the Far East, but also societies nearer to our own, such as more remote areas of Europe, and even our own society. This is the *archaeology of ourselves* or, as it is now fashionably called, Modern Material Culture – MMC.

While modern ethnoarchaeologists are still interested in examining the life of modern hunter-gatherers and asking the simple question, 'could hunter-gatherers in Europe in 20,000 BC have been living in similar ways?', their motivation is rather more complex. The reasons for doing ethnoarchaeology may be summed up as follows:

89

(1) To record material culture – tools, building types, technical devices, clothing, food-processing equipment, beds, boats, mills, agricultural practices – which are fast disappearing under the onslaught of industrialization and mass communication. This is intrinsically interesting on its own account, and will be much more so for posterity, whatever use we or they may make of these data. Currently most of such recording is by writing, photographing and drawing, with some use of a tape-recorder or video-camera.

(2) To study the relationship between material culture and human behaviour, since in living societies we can ascertain what human beings are doing (or appear to be doing), and very often why they are doing it (if we can believe them!) We can see what is the by-product – the rubbish – which arises out of human behaviour. We can consider how its patterns (for example, the way rubbish is distributed around a house) are the result of what is happening in the society. Patterns of artefacts may have arisen through wholly functional behaviour (for example, rubbish being kept away from sleeping areas) or through more subtle cosmological beliefs. For instance, in one African society, the very plan of the family house is anthropomorphic – one end is regarded as the 'head' (where males work), the other is the 'excretory' end (where the females work). All rubbish must be kept at this end and not round the head, as in the living body. While not flattering to females, this is the explanation for the distribution of rubbish which an archaeologist might later find.

(3) To test the traditional inferences about such relationships which may have been generated in archaeological theory, and to build up a body of new archaeological theory which will help in the interpretation of the remains of long extinct peoples. Note the difference between this approach and the older one of saying 'here in this cave we have the debris of hunter-gatherers of the end of the last Ice Age. The debris bears striking resemblance to this African hunter-gatherer group that we are now studying; therefore our prehistoric group lived as they do.'

An example of this is the classic case of Millie's Camp (Bonnichsen, 1973). This was a trappers' camp in the Canadian Rockies used by indigenous Indians. Archaeologists came across it a few weeks after it had been abandoned. There were the remains of shelters, hearths, traps, appliances, tree carvings, clothing, waste material, food and drink wrappers, cosmetics, toys, tobacco tins, and some odd patterns of things which looked very 'ritual'. The 177 'finds' included a label from Rider Cowboy jeans, plastic hair curlers, a Dinky toy Land Rover, a yellow toy parachute jumper, the arms of a white plastic toy skeleton, a Kodak film wrapper, bags from Robin Hood Quick Oats and Aunt Jemima pancake mix, and pages from *Eaton's Catalogue*. The archaeologists made a detailed plan and catalogue, and, using established archaeological principles of inference, wrote a report on such matters as local resources, 'activity areas', the size of the family and its composition, how many people, what sex, their economy, their technology, religion and lifestyle, and how long they had been there. They then went into town, and found and talked to Millie, who had been one of the camp's inhabitants. She was surprised, co-operative, amused, and articulate when she learnt that the archaeologists wanted to know the whole 'truth' about the camp. She accompanied them back to the site, and gave them a complete run-down on exactly who was who, what was what, and what had been going on there. The archaeologists were, of course, wrong in almost every respect. But they were now able to make a formal comparison between their own 'model' of life at Millie's camp and as it really was, and see where and how their basic inferences were wrong. Next time they interpreted the remains found on an archaeological site of prehistoric Canadian trapper-hunters, they were presumably more cautious, sadder, and wiser men.

Their experience is directly related to our final category:

(4) The expanding of mental horizons. People used to travel to widen their cultural horizons. A lot of people now travel, see nothing, attempt to understand nothing, and come back as ignorant as they went. When archaeologists travel, they see and observe, and their whole store of knowledge and understanding increases. In looking at the material culture of other countries we

can, *as students* – not necessarily as researchers – learn an enormous amount which we could not learn by staying at home (even by watching TV programmes about distant places). We can learn about many different ways of doing things – ploughing with oxen or camels, building wooden houses, making objects in wood or metal, preparing and cooking food, how primitive machinery functions, how land is irrigated, how fish are caught, how boats are made, how a windmill works, how butter and cheese are made, how the entire economy of an island runs, and how people interact with the forces of nature.

## ETHNOARCHAEOLOGY AROUND THE MEDITERRANEAN

I have chosen these examples deliberately – they are not what one would learn by living with New Guinea farmers, or trekking with Aborigines. They are things that can be seen in Europe, notably in Greece, Turkey, Yugoslavia, Spain and (just across the Straits) in Morocco. These are poor countries where, in more remote areas, modern things like tractors and refrigerators are beyond many people's means. They are places where the material culture is archaic, the technology and economy primitive by Western European standards.

The things we see are more akin to what medieval Britain must have been like in many ways. Thus the medieval archaeologist like myself, or any archaeologist who seeks a wider understanding of how things work, can widen his or her own cultural experience of such things enormously. Life in present-day Britain or America gives us little insight into what things were like in the past. We can read books, we can talk to very old people, but we can also travel and see these things *being done*.

It would be simplistic to say, 'here is village life in a high mountain area of northern Spain; there is no electricity, mains water, gas or cars; everything is done by hand: *therefore* this is what life must have been like in a Yorkshire village in the fourteenth century.' Yet after seeing the Spanish village, one has more insight into what life in any rural community may be like, *at that level of technology*. We can also say that pictures of peasant life depicted in loving detail in the fourteenth-century Luttrell Psalter are remarkably like scenes one can witness in Turkey or Morocco (given different climates, clothing and people's faces).

What I am stressing is that ethnoarchaeology at this *educational*, relatively simple level is not an abstruse academic topic, as my categories (2) and (3) above are. Anyone can observe and learn in category (4), and with a little experience anyone can join in category (1) of ethnoarchaeology and *record*.

### ETHNOARCHAEOLOGY ON THE CHEAP

To do such work in Europe it is not necessary to have major research funds or elaborately equipped expeditions. It is cheap, and within everybody's reach. It can make a holiday a stimulating and educational experience, rather than just lying in the sun, swimming, drinking, or finding the nearest discotheque (the four main attractions figured in holiday brochures).

In the last part of this chapter, I will describe some of the ethnoarchaeology that my wife and I have done in recent years, and how it is related to my four categories of motivation or justification outlined above. The reader may not be convinced that our experience has been very academic, but our basic enjoyment of it will, I hope, be clear.

Even the package holiday-makers see something of the different cultures of high sun/low rainfall areas. Excursions take them to local markets, but their preoccupation is principally with picking up some cheap bargain of leather or textile. If they notice the 'natives', it is not with respect or even curiosity, and they certainly wouldn't like them to marry their sons and daughters. Yet much can be seen in ordinary holiday areas, often within five or ten kilometres of the Costa Brava, the Costa del Sol or, further afield, in the coastal resorts of Turkey, in the Greek Islands or anywhere along the North African coast. Much of what is to be seen and observed is of course directly relevant to our understanding of the antiquity of classical times, Byzantium or Islam, but it is also very educational in more general ways to an archaeologist of northern Europe.

### CATEGORIES OF STUDY IN ETHNOARCHAEOLOGY

My examples are classified under seven main headings, all related to the reasons for doing ethnoarchaeology outlined above. These are: (a) appreciation of basic land-forms, geology, topography, climate: environmental archaeology; (b) understanding of the economy of areas or whole countries, often unchanged for hundreds of years, if now rapidly being abandoned north of the Mediterranean, and how that economy is interwoven with social life and custom; (c) the archaeology of subsistence, arable and pastoral farming, marine resources, and the vast areas still given over to those staples of classical times, the grape and the olive; (d) technology, archaic kinds of machinery, sometimes also going back to the first millennium AD: the threshing 'machine', wheeled or pack transport and (of especial interest to us) the watermill; (e) daily life in remote communities: homes, food preparation and cooking; (f) mortuary behaviour: the archaeology of death and burial; and (g) religion, ritual and value systems.

## The environment

It's important for an archaeologist to understand the environment and people's interaction with it (Butzer, 1982). One can observe the land-forms, geology, water and climate, and note the ways in which these determine the resources available in an area at any time, the subsistence strategies, and what types of surplus are likely to be available for exchanging for things which cannot be locally produced. Archaeologists of the post-classical period have noted massive deposits of soil and stones which fill valleys and estuaries, dated to the seventh–eighth centuries AD (Vita-Finzi, 1969). This 'younger fill', as it is called, has been attributed to the breakdown of the classical civilization. There was no longer a market for agricultural produce, the field revetments or retaining walls were neglected, and heavy winter rains washed out the soil that had been so carefully accumulated for centuries before.

The same kind of thing can be seen happening today, but for

very different reasons. Many of the old terraced fields of the Mediterranean coastal areas are being abandoned to grass or scrub, as their owners gradually sell out to speculative builders; the farms are falling into ruin, the field edges being broken down, and the soil washing out in the winter rains and the flood-water from the melting snows of the mountains.

## The economy

Away from the coasts of the Mediterranean, many of the older exchange systems are still operating. Country produce – vegetables, fruit, wine – floods into towns like Madrid or Rome, in what is today a money economy. Country towns act as nuclei for rural areas around them, providing markets, judiciary and banking systems and other 'central place' facilities. This is not so strange to British observes, as much of this kind of system operates in Britain. In North Africa, however, earlier systems of more direct exchange are still operating, which are more like those of medieval Europe.

In Morocco, there are a few large cities which act only partly as central places; they all have different functions in the country as a whole. Tangier is the gateway to the Mediterranean, a cosmopolitan port. Casablanca is the principal port for the importation of industrial products from northern Europe: this is where you (or a wholesaler) go to buy a car, a washing machine or a television. Rabat is the centre of government, where the king lives, where the National Museum is to be found (and very interesting it is), where the army has its headquarters. Fez is the centre of culture and learning, with its arts and crafts specialists; its university is one of the oldest in Europe, several centuries older than Oxford or Cambridge. Finally, Marrakesh is a great rural centre for the Berber areas of the Atlas mountains.

Marrakesh, a good deal further south than the other 'functional' cities, is the only one of these that has as its primary role that of a great nucleus of exchange and social concourse. In the early hours of the morning lorries converge on the city, bringing in goods from a wide radius. By late morning, many thousands of people are thronging the markets and enjoying themselves in the enormous 'square'. This has been called a 'permanent seven-ring circus'. Here, every day, there are groups of musicians, dancers, performing animals, reciters from the Koran, magicians and con-jurers, blind beggars, water-sellers, purveyors of aphrodisiacs and strange herbs and remedies, drug-peddlers, crooks and pick-pockets from both sides of the Sahara. To watch this scene is to give oneself some inkling of what it must have been like to be in a great medieval or classical city. Tourists are in a very small minority in Marrakesh and mostly, like us, pretty frightened people!

More typical, perhaps, of the medieval or earlier rural eco-nomy are the very small country towns of Morocco which act solely as market centres. As one approaches one of these in the morning, one can see converging on it, from country areas ten or twenty kilometres around, lines of donkeys or camels laden with many different kinds of produce – tomatoes, figs, grapes, oranges, eggs, salt, fowl, honey, goats. During the day there is much haggling and direct exchange, in which money plays a relatively minor role, and in the later afternoon the same pack-animals wend their way back into the hills and valleys with what they have bought or exchanged. The town here provides the location of the market and services – money changers, eating-places, hairdressers, a relatively small permanent population. There are also open markets at strategic points, which operate on certain days of the week; here too are the hundreds of stalls, rows of hairdressers, and purveyors of snacks, but at sundown all is packed away and the place is deserted.

The archaeologist observes with interest this socioeconomic life: the systems that underlie what is being seen, the structures of certain kinds of site and activities and the patterns of rubbish disposal that result. Here the archaeologist is taking a rather different view from a socioeconomist. The latter will also be observing not only these relatively archaic ways of life, but also how they are changing (especially north of the Mediterranean) under the impact of western industrialization, notably the influence of motorized transport, new roads, cash-crops and tourism.

*Subsistence*

The agricultural economy can be studied in a wide variety of locations. The most widespread archaeological and landscape feature in all parts of southern Europe are the terraced fields, constructed at great expense of labour to build the revetment walls to retain the precious soil and facilitate irrigation, another major feature of classical and Arab farming. Although large areas of these are now abandoned, many more survive in use, yielding a wide variety of crops. Here can be seen in operation systems of small fields very like the so-called 'celtic' fields which until recently survived as earthworks so dramatically in the chalk downlands of southern England. They are rapidly now being bulldozed away for modern, larger-scale farming.

In arable areas, one can see ard-ploughs very similar to those in use in Iron Age or Roman Britain. They are being pulled by oxen (as in fourteenth-century England) by donkeys, mules, horses or camels, or even (in Morocco) very oddly by a camel and a donkey in tandem!

Sowing is still done in many areas by 'broadcasting' by hand from a basket (as in the Luttrell Psalter and the Bible), and reaping by hand, either by a sickle or by pulling the whole root out. All this is very labour intensive, as it was in pre-modern times in northern Europe. Threshing floors, circular flat areas, often with a retaining wall, are a very common feature still in Turkey, Greece, Spain and Portugal. The corn was broken up either by animals being led round and round the floor, or by animals pulling a sledge, whose front curved up, and whose underside was studded with sharp-edged flints or other stones. This *tribulum* is a direct descendant of the threshing sledge known by that name in classical times. We saw the *tribulum* at work work in northern Spain (Leon) and brought part of one back to York. It had been abandoned and thrown on a wood heap (we paid 100 pesetas for this, about 60p). We wedged it into the roof of the Land Rover and it now graces the hall of the department in York, where it can be studied at leisure.

Large areas of southern Europe are still given over to the olive and grape. The olive plantation trees, some covering thousands of hectares in mid-Spain, are said to be direct descendants of the Roman ones. The importance of wine in classical and medieval times can hardly be overestimated; Mediterranean wine was being imported into Britain and Ireland from the Iron Age onwards (witnessed by finds of pottery *amphorae*) and one can still see the whole process of viticulture in virtually every European country south of Denmark.

## Technology

I have already mentioned the threshing device, the *tribulum*, now being ousted by the threshing machine proper. Our main interests in the field of technology have been in irrigation, and in the related techniques of milling, the final process in the arable economy. Windmills and vertical-wheeled watermills are still to be found, though increasingly rarely in working order, in northern Europe, but *horizontal*-wheeled mills are different.

I excavated one of only two Anglo-Saxon watermills known in England, at Tamworth in the Midlands, dated to the middle of the ninth century (Rahtz and Meeson, forthcoming). The remains were relatively well preserved for such an ancient structure (due to waterlogging), and we became interested in this primitive kind of mill, its origins and the exact way it worked, in order to understand our archaeological evidence from Tamworth better. This kind of mill now survives only in the southern Mediterranean and in the far north. It was to the south that we went in search of these. Our first field-work here was in Crete. We recorded details of several dozen ruined examples, but at last found two in complete working order, still earning their living grinding corn for the local community. Most of the mills we saw dated from the sixteenth–nineteenth centuries, but we had an invaluable insight into how such mills worked. We subsequently published a paper on the Cretan mills, and we have since then recorded horizontal-wheeled mills in south west France, the Pyrenees, Turkey, southern Spain, the Canaries, and especially in northern Spain, in Galicia. Here, in a short tour, we found several examples still working, and this is probably the region where most survive in Europe today, in an area where water is very plentiful (Rahtz, 1981).

Another technology which was common in medieval Europe, but now survives in its old form only in the south, is pottery making, firing and selling. We have seen the entire process in traditional pottery-making areas in Spain and elsewhere, giving us an invaluable model for the medieval pottery manufacture in Britain.

## Daily life

Peasants, and the peasant way of life, long extinct in northern Europe, are still common enough in the south. Electricity, plastics, TV, piped water and cars are rapidly changing country ways of life, but a great deal survives. One doesn't have to travel very far from tourist resorts to see grain being made into flour by a hand quern; butter being made by 'throwing' the buttermilk around in a bag made from a goat's stomach; shepherds in high mountains making soft cheese from goats' milk (using calor gas, however!) and bringing their cheese down to the local market every Saturday; hand spinning, fulling and weaving; and people milking animals by hand, using carts with solid wooden wheels, riding on pack-animals, and engaged in a wide variety of food preparation and cooking. All of these activities are familiar to the archaeologist through the material debris they leave behind, and in these places one can see all details of the activities which produce such artifacts.

In the south Spanish province of Almeria, in a small sheltered valley, there are terraced fields, a threshing floor, a spring and washing place, a small gorge, palm trees and huge cacti. In this garden-like landscape are a group of four or five farms, mostly abandoned in the late 1950s and not yet taken over for the white-stuccoed 'pueblo'-type villas of rich aliens.

The impression one gets from a recently deserted landscape of this kind is that this is what Britain must have looked like in the sixth century, with numerous ruined or semi-ruined buildings about, many of the fields reverting to scrub, hedges, revetments, water-supplies and drainage neglected; and a marked population drop in rural areas. Oddly enough, the inheritors and improvers of the neglected landscape of Roman Britain and this part of southern Spain were the same people – the English – though for very different reasons!

In those farmhouses that have been abandoned, much of the material culture has been left behind, presumably because it is of such little value if one is moving to a new apartment block in a nearby town. Thus both houses and contents are still there, rather as if the inhabitants had died of the plague. We made a plan of one of the farmhouses, and noted all the details of materials, construction and use of the space; all the rooms were numbered and the function of each worked out. We made an inventory of all the objects lying around in each room: iron-bound wooden chests, old broken chairs and tables, baskets and other containers of sisal-weave; bottles, tins, ceramic dishes, a 'dead' bicycle, feather-mattresses, carved wooden beds, a string of garlic, hay, animal manure, a plough-beam and share, and many others. These objects of course belong to someone; they cannot be removed, only listed and photographed. Even if we don't use these data for any direct archaeological analogue, we are recording an example of material culture that will not survive where such farms continue in use, as modern materials fast supersede the old. This, it should be noted, is ten minutes' walk from one of the most popular tourist hotels on the south coast of Spain.

One of the archaeologist's most common finds is pottery, which has been made all over the world in an extraordinary variety of fabric, form and function. As already mentioned, we have studied pottery making. We have also bought local ceramics in many countries in Europe. They now form a remarkable 'ethnographic collection', which can used to illustrate the appearane of classical *amphorae* or medieval costrels, fish-dishes or jugs, for these things have changed very little.


## Death and burial

This subject lends itself very much to ethnoarchaeology. For the archaeologist, the dead are one of the most important sources of evidence, for their skeletons, coffins and grave goods. All these survive in varying degrees, but little remains of the wider aspects of death in society – the events leading up to the funeral, the funeral itself, and the major ripples in society that death causes. All these can of course be observed in modern society, to see what material remains might be found in favourable circumstances.

Death and burial is a subject that has received a lot of attention on a world-wide basis by archaeologists, from the earliest Stone Age burials through barrows, cists, tombs, burial ships, pyramids and cremations to the millions of graves in cemeteries; from the richly furnished, jade-suited Chinese princesses of the second century BC to the modern public cemetery and the horrors of the American funeral industry.

One of my most successful (if rather ghoulish) lectures is on the 'archaeology of modern death', the material culture that surrounds death today: from the infrastructure of the undertaking industry, with its flowers, hearses and embalmers, to the funeral feasts and mourning dress and, especially, the rich source of grave memorials. I gathered the material for this lecture from many different ethnoarchaeological contexts. I have photographed a funeral in Sicily, 'cities of the dead' in the Mediterranean, the hundreds of clothed mummified bodies in the Capuchin crypt at Palermo, Islamic graves in Istanbul and the Atlas mountains, hearses in Spain and funeral notices in Greece.

One of the best-known examples of ethnoarchaeology is the study of New England gravestones of the eighteenth and nineteenth centuries. Since every one is precisely dated, the patterns of changing form and symbolism in town and country areas can be exactly plotted. The changes from death's heads to cherubs to willow and urn can be seen in their beginnings in urban centres like Boston or Plymouth (where the 'fashions' arrived from Europe), gradually diffusing into country areas. This analysis gives a perfect model of the way such diffusion works, and has been used to check inferences about similar changes in form and symbolism in prehistory.

The wider our knowledge of modern death and burial, the more may we hope to understand the wide variety of mortuary behaviour we encounter in the ancient world. Why, for instance, do some people cremate, others bury, and yet others throw bodies in rivers or leave them out to be eaten? Why is cremation becoming more and more popular in today's Western Europe? What is the relationship between wealth and social status and the form or ostentation of grave or memorial?

### Religion, ritual and value systems

This is too big a topic to deal with adequately in a short space. Archaeology is notoriously bad at being able to deduce the nature of early religious belief (we don't even know what Stonehenge 'means') or even much of what went on in people's minds. Comparative religion in the world today is very much a subject for anthropologists or theologians. All that archaeologists can do is to watch and observe and think – 'what would I make of all this if I found it in a ruin?' The reader is invited for a moment to be a Martian archaeologist excavating the ruins of our destroyed civilization. What would you make of a large building that is oriented east–west, that has no occupation dirt around it, and where all the nourishment seems to be a bottle of wine and some wafers. There is a special table-like structure at the east end, and a sort of shallow bath on a stand at the other. There is a good deal of imagery of a rather violent kind, of someone nailed to a cross etc. *We* know it's a Christian church and *we* know what all these things symbolize, but to an alien archaeologist it would be very puzzling. Hence our total incomprehension when faced with Indian or Far Eastern religious practice today.

On a more prosaic level, one ethnoarchaeological observation of religious practice did something to increase our confidence in the 'ritual' or religious character of a find some 1500 years earlier.

At Cadbury-Congresbury, in Somerset, we excavated a small pit of the sixth century AD, a 'Dark Age' site in Britain. In this pit was an odd assortment of bits of pot, metal objects, flints, slag, bone and glass waste, some eighty objects in all. It looked as if someone had deliberately gone round the site in the sixth century AD and gathered together a sample of everything that was around. Virtually everything we found in a large excavation was represented in this pit. Sealed beneath the rock lining were some weathered fragments of human skull (there were no other burials on the site). Was all this 'ritual' (a word used by archaeologists when they don't understand what they have found)? If so, was it Christian or pagan (it could be either in this time and place)? Were the skull fragments something rather gruesome that the pit succeeded? Could we cite any ethnoarchaeological parallels for such a 'domestic assemblage' having a 'religious' interpretation?

The answer came soon afterwards when we were in a very remote part of Europe, the west coast of County Donegal in Ireland. Close to where we stayed was a holy well, part of an early Christian complex possibly itself more ancient. But the holy well was still, as often in Ireland, a place of Christian visitation. Around the little pool of water in a rock-cleft (which is all the well was) was an astonishing collection of objects – bits of clothing, combs, biros, a plastic magnifying glass, two religious tracts on holy water and happiness wrapped in paper bags, a collection of pre-decimal (valueless) coins in a purse; a hair-slide, and some more obviously Christian objects such as crosses and china Madonnas (one in a bottle). In a small cave close by were dozens more objects of the same kind, and bottles of all kinds from shampoo to detergent. In the mouth of the cave (which a small child might have crawled into) was a stone shaped like an old-fashioned bun-loaf, slightly anthropomorphic, but clearly natural. We photographed and listed these objects without moving them, classifying them by their material and original function. Discreet enquiry elicited the facts that all these objects were either associated with someone whose illness it was hoped to cure, or with someone who had been cured. The stone was a healing stone, used to effect a cure by being placed over the affected part. So potent was it, it was said, that it had been to America twice to cure Irish exiles. Someone had once thrown it into the sea, but it reappeared in the cave the next day. We later published all this (Rahtz and Watts, 1979) as a piece of ethno-archaeology of especial interest. It did not enable us to say that our sixth century pit *was* likewise a ritual feature, but it did show that it *could* have been. It wasn't entirely ridiculous to suggest that such a collection was religious, because we could now quote an *ethnoarchaeological parallel.*

In discussing the ethnoarchaeology of value systems, we will look at rubbish and dirt. The English tourist in southern Europe is appalled by the way 'the locals' spread rubbish everywhere, especially in remote or beautiful country or coast areas. The wilder the place, the more one is likely to find dumps of plastic, glass and tin in places where there is no chance of it being collected by public garbage collection. In former times when most rubbish was organic it didn't matter so much, as it all rotted away. Now it doesn't, and the result to us is a major eyesore, not to mention the health hazards and dangers to children and animals. Our observation has been, however, that the locals *don't mind.* The wild areas are places beyond the areas that are useful – fields, bars, homes, gardens, work-places – and appropriate therefore for disposal of rubbish. Now that social custom has persuaded, for example, the Spaniards that the wild, especially the coastal spot, is a suitable place to drive to on a Sunday, some change might be expected, but it is not happening; they are apparently oblivious to it. It is part of their value system; their attitude to dirt is not ours. Yet repeatedly we apply our own value judgements when we find dumps of dirt on floors, or round entrances or down wells. We decide that this must be the work of 'squatters' rather than the 'proper' inhabitants, and start to think of suitable historical settings, of conquest or the collapse of political authority.

Finally, a piece of ethnoarchaeology that was not directly related to the past, but wholly to the material culture of present-day Christian centres: as part of a trip to northern Spain and the past-related agricultural and milling technology, we visited Lourdes and Santiago de Compostela. Although both these sites are important present-day pilgrimage centres, Lourdes in particular attracting over two million visitors a year, they are very different. Lourdes, in southwest France, is barely a hundred years old as a shrine, the site of St Bernadette's visions. Santiago de Compostela in northwest Spain has been a pilgrim centre since the ninth century AD, and is the reputed burial place of St James.

There are many other contrasts in the material culture, notably in the souvenirs sold for pilgrims to take home as witness of their visit. This is a custom that was very common in medieval times, pilgrim badges being worn on hat or cloak. The badge associated with St James is a scallop shell; this is the symbol all along the route, on signposts and other objects. The symbols for Lourdes are St Bernadette and the Virgin in the grotto of the visions. The souvenirs at Lourdes are an industry. The streets (but not the grotto) are more like Blackpool or Coney Island than a holy city. Every conceivable object that can be decorated with St Bernadette and the Virgin is sold in thousands, ranging from plastic bottles for collecting the holy water to hats, from biscuits to household shrines, lit by electricity. They are sold in dozens of very vulgar shops with notices such as 'Tourisme et Religion'. We made an inventory and classification of the objects at both places (Santiago is much less obtrusive) rather as we had for the Irish holy well (Rahtz and Watts, 1986.)

The interest here is the extent to which such assemblages of the modern material culture of religions change. Earlier visitors to Lourdes described the vulgarity of the scene, but must have seen rather different range from those on sale in the 1980s. Similarly, a visitor in the year 2000 will find it interesting to compare our list with what is available then. Since Lourdes has been well documented from its inception by written accounts and photographs, it would be possible to relate all the changes to changing styles of pilgrimage, relative wealth, social habits and, especially, available material, and develop archaeological theory accordingly.

CONCLUSIONS

I hope that all readers of this chapter will now go on their holidays with a more observant and less prejudiced eye, and will be able to avoid the boredom of the beaches. For our next chapter we turn to more light relief, the fringe areas of archaeology, perhaps suitable to be read *on* beaches as it was, after all, written on one!

# 7

# Fringe Archaeology

## HUMOUR IN ARCHAEOLOGY

Archaeologists can be serious people, some too much so. But many have a keen sense of humour, and when seen *en masse* at conferences and excursions can be a very jolly crowd. Archaeology, it might be paraphrased, is too important a subject *not* to be joked about. I insert jokes into lectures as a way of keeping my audience awake. The trouble is that they remember the jokes, but not the rest of the lecture, so the jokes have to be *important* jokes which illustrate profound truths about something or other.

Archaeological humour can be at the expense of archaeologists. No one has yet gathered up all the jokes about archaeology, though there are a few collections. Cartoons especially, in *Punch*, the *New Yorker* and elsewhere, are a valuable source for the study of changing social attitudes to archaeology. There are certain stock situations: bearded professors in topees in Egyptian tombs figure prominently, as do encounters with skeletons. They reflect popular misunderstandings about our work, which will only be eradicated when archaeology becomes part of the school curriculum.

One of my favourite jokes, which I have told hundreds of times, embodies a profound contrast in philosophical attitudes, and neatly sums up the contrast between what archaeologists do, and what other people think they do:

*Yorkshire farmer* (to Oxford archaeologist digging in trench):
　　'Ave yer found owt?' (for our non-English readers this is
　　　　Yorkshire for: 'Have you found anything?')
*Oxford archaeologist*:
　　(looking up) 'I beg your pardon?'
*YF*: 'I said, 'ave yer found owt?'
*OA*: (still puzzled)
　　'Have I found out *what*?'


　　The humour that this chapter deals with is not, however, that of the outside world about archaeologists, ancient peoples, dinosaurs and ancient monuments, but that of archaeologists about themselves or their subject.


## How likely is likely?

I begin by reproducing a short piece I wrote some years ago. It was written in half an hour as a fringe item at a local conference, but, because it expressed some fundamental truths *and* was quite funny, it was published. This short piece has been quoted more often than the major reports I've written, which is rather galling!

　　Modern archaeologists are constantly urging the necessity for a stricter and more scientific use of language and logic in archaeology. Some archaeological interpretations are based on such poor evidence in the ground that one can only say that the conclusion is 'possible, though very unlikely'; others are so positive as to be 'very probable, amounting almost to certainty'. Between these two extremes lies a range of quality of evidence which is infinite in its diversity both in kind and degree. Can the range be quantified? Windstrengths are given a ten-point (Beaufort) scale based on measurable characteristics. While archaeological evidence has more diversity than windstrengths, is it possible to erect a ten-point scale ranging from quality 1 (very unlikely) to 10 (certain), which can be linked with written equivalents?

　　We set it out thus:

| Probability scale | Literary equivalent |
|:---:|:---|
| 1 | Very unlikely |
| 2 | Unlikely |
| 3 | Possible |
| 4 | Very possible |
| 5 | Likely |
| 6 | More than likely |
| 7 | Probable |
| 8 | Very probable |
| 9 | Virtually certain |
| 10 | Certain |

The more 'elegant' archaeological reports are littered with dozens of such phrases used to express subtle nuances of degrees of probability. Are they used as sober assessments of the evidence; or as elements of rhetoric to persuade the reader to one subjective opinion on what the evidence can bear? The use of a scale might force archaeologists to think more carefully about what weight the evidence will bear. Too often, the choice of the elegant phrase covers up a vague and woolly approach to the evidence; in the best of hands it will of course express half-tones of delicate balance between this and that which simply cannot be quantified. This is a valid technique if its object is to direct the reader's attention to the evidence itself, a challenging invitation to decide for him or herself just how likely the claim made is.

Unfortunately, few writers of archaeological reports are skilful in the use of words, even if they do in fact fully appreciate what can and what cannot be deduced from the evidence in the ground. If they do not have the gift of words, they might do better to use a number scale; their readers would then at least know how likely *they* thought was likely!

Even worse, some writers are more concerned with converting readers to their point of view than with expounding a balanced estimate of the validity of the evidence. To do this, they use literary techniques which are misleading or even dishonest in a 'scientific' report. They do in fact create an *inverse* scale of probability. Discerning readers will see through this, and apply a reversal factor; others will be persuaded. Examples of such an inverse scale might run thus (the 'modesty' of the first example is as misleading as the persuasiveness of the rest):

| Phrase | Actual meaning |
| --- | --- |
| 'Just possible' | I'm pretty certain but I can't actually prove it; the reader will see how cautious and clever I'm being |
| 'There is some evidence pointing towards ...' | There isn't any but it would be nice if there were |
| 'The evidence suggests that ...' | If it were twisted beyond recognition |
| 'It is reasonable to suggest that ...' | It is unreasonable but I may persuade my readers to believe it by an appeal to their reasonableness |
| 'Virtually certain' | I'm on very shaky ground here |
| 'There can be no doubt that ...' (or more commonly) 'doubtless' | Anybody who disagrees will feel a fool |
| 'Plausible' | Well, ever so interesting if it were true |
| 'It would be premature to suggest' | But wouldn't it be fun |
| 'All the evidence taken together points to ...' | It all points in different directions |
| 'Obviously', 'indisputably', or 'presumably' | There is no actual evidence |
| 'No right-thinking scholar can doubt' or 'the discerning reader will observe ...' | These are my final trump cards |

These dubious phrases about the quality of evidence should put the discerning reader on guard, but an ability to 'translate' other statements found in archaeological reports is also needed. For example:

| Phrase | Actual meaning |
| --- | --- |
| 'Further research may indicate . . .' | Mine certainly doesn't |
| 'Adverse excavation conditions . . .' | The recording was terrible |
| 'There was no evidence of . . .' | If there was, we didn't see it |
| 'The object crumbled into dust on exposure to the air . . .' | Joe sat on it |
| 'The relationship between these layers was uncertain . . .' | Joe dug it away when we weren't looking |
| 'The date of the end of the occupation of the villa was shown by the latest coins, which were of Honorius . . .' (see next pages) | I don't believe in all this Dark Age nonsense |
| 'A scatter of small stones associated with two handmade sherds . . .' | I do |
| 'It was not possible . . .' | We didn't think of it till afterwards |
| 'A flimsy structure . . .' | Moira planned the post-holes |

## The end of Roman Britain

One short piece was written directly for inclusion in a lecture on 'The End of Roman Britain', because I could think of no better way of making a point, and making it memorable (alas!) by personalization. The point was to expose a major fallacy found in much archaeological writing about this period. This is that the dating of the latest levels in (say) a Roman villa is given by the dating of the latest coins found in that deposit, or by the date of manufacture of the pottery found. Since coins ceased to reach this country very soon after *c.* AD 400, and Roman pottery manufacture did not long survive this breakdown in a monetary economy, these objects can only give a *date after which* the latest occupation took place, which might be fifty, a hundred or two hundred years after those dates. At a conservative estimate, there were twenty million pots in use in Roman Britain in AD 400; they didn't all get broken in a resounding smash soon after that date; and those that survived became even more valuable.

A related fallacy is that when archaeologists find that the latest levels are full of 'dirt' – bones, potsherds, oyster shells, dead dogs, with fires being lit on mosaic pavements – they attribute these remains to 'squatters', rather than to long-drawn-out secondary usage of the building by people with different life-styles or purposes. These points are brought out in the following fable:

Marcus, a late Romano-Briton, was living in an urban environment in AD 400 with his wife Calpurnia and their two young children Festus and Priscilla. Discussion round their dinner table was similar to that of today – impending doom and a feeling that civilized life as they knew it was not going to survive the adulthood of their children. Marcus was already remarking that the pottery stalls in the market were not so packed, or with so much variety, as they were when he was a boy, and his grandfather had told him that what pottery there was lacked the elegance of earlier days. He had indeed inherited a samian bowl, but it was never used, being now an antique and kept on a shelf and showed round only on ancestor day.

After a few more years had passed, he returned from the market one day with the news that he had not been able to buy a new black-burnished cooking pot which Calpurnia had asked him to get. He'd been told by old Sextus the pottery-stall keeper that he hadn't been able to get any – they weren't making them any more – it was getting too difficult to market them and there was no profit in it. They looked round somewhat sadly at the rows of pots on the kitchen shelves, which had suddenly acquired a new value. 'You'd better not break any more', he ruefully told her. They counted them up – there were thirty-five of them of various sizes, from dish to storage jar.

By AD 420, twenty had been broken, both by the clumsiness of the ageing and arthritic Calpurnia and also by her lively grandchildren; and now that it was clear that the potters were not going to resume production, each loss occasioned a terrible family row.

By AD 440 both Marcus and Calpurnia were dead, and the house and pottery had passed into the hands of their son, Festus, now himself approaching middle age, with two grown-up children. Because of their increasing rarity value, the breaking rate had dropped; five more pots had gone by AD 440, leaving ten surviving.

Twenty years later, on a dark November afternoon in AD 460, the now aged widower Festus was sitting by the fire, dreaming of the old days of central heating by hypocaust which he dimly remembered as a boy. There was a noise outside the back door and then it suddenly burst open, and two uncouth, hairy toughs stormed into the room, gabbling in some guttural tongue. Old Festus jumped up and protested, but was silenced by a mortal blow. The intruders knocked down everything in sight, the samian bowl smashed on the floor, and so did the other ten pots. The old man staggered away to die, and the toughs set fire to the house after eating all the food they could find.

Fifteen hundred years passed, and an archaeologist began work on this area. He found the broken pottery on the floor, and noted in his diary that this was clearly the 'behavioural residue' of the latest 'squatter' occupation of the house, albeit rather 'squalid' (since the invaders had left chicken bones and oyster shells of their last meal on the floor too). When the dig was finished, the archaeologist studied the pottery and looked up parallels for fabric and form. Surprise, surprise, they were all mid- to late-fourth century – the samian was of course 'residual', whatever that means. In the report we duly find 'the final phase was rather squalid; the associated pottery dated this occupation to the later fourth century, a conclusion confirmed by the coin sequence in the area, which also ends with issues of Valentinian II and Honorius' (late fourth century).

## The alternative abbey

My next example derives from our excavations at Bordesley Abbey. In some dirt in the choir area of the church, we found a small ivory dice. This immediately conjured up ideas of gambling within the church during long, boring masses, and of generally lax discipline in the monastery. The idea was rather reinforced by finding chicken bones in the dirt under the choir-stalls: a surreptitious snack. Out of this, in the teatime break, grew a whole alternative scenario – a life at Bordesley Abbey which the abbot didn't know about. This was 'realized' on a blackboard by Ian Burrow, an inveterate archaeologist/joker, and although it was ephemeral in this form, I did luckily take a photograph of it. I later realized that it could be used to illustrate in a memorable way what we mean when we talk of the contrast between the way institutions *appear* to operate, the 'public' image, and what goes on in reality, a matter of interest to both sociologists, anthropologists and archaeologists. Figure 5 was the result.

As a postscript to this, I read in the *Statistics* volume in this series (Kennedy, 1983, page 57) that dice were used by medieval monks to help them decide which virtue should be specially practised that day; so we had probably maligned our Bordesley monks.

## Humour in the history of archaeology

Much archaeological humour, including the above examples, is a product of its day, and may quickly become dated, like *Punch* cartoons of the last century. It does nevertheless have some relevance in the history of the archaeology of the period, a social by-product of a kind which it would be difficult to infer from the academic publications of the same period.

Some of the items above verge on fantasy and are also perhaps related to science-fiction. This can also be humorous, but has a potentially more important role, which will be discussed in the next section.

*Figure 5*  A structuralist approach to Bordesley Abbey

## SCIENCE–FICTION AND ACADEMIA

Science-fiction is now a respectable academic topic. One can get a degree in it in at least one American institution, and the University of York recently ran an open course on the subject; the lecturers considered the relationship of SF to history, language, sociology, theology, science and pseudo-science. They demonstrated the ways in which SF was able to bring a new dimension to each subject; the lecturer giving 'SF and Theology' claimed, for example (and very plausibly), that SF had done more for comparative theology in its explorations of alternative religions than had the academics in theology departments.

### The importance of archaeological SF

Archaeology did not figure in this series of lectures, but there is no doubt of SF's importance here in expanding the horizons of an archaeologist's mind, even more than the ethnoarchaeology discussed in chapter 6. No one has yet surveyed the whole field of archaeology in SF, and this book is not the place to do it. All I can do here is to indicate briefly the modes of treatment archaeology has had or might have from SF writers. Most of that written is relatively uninformed, and little has been written by archaeologists themselves.

SF is a remedy against parochialism, anthropocentrism and too easy cultural assumptions. Much archaeology practised in Britain is Anglocentric, or at best Eurocentric. The archaeology of the Far East, Polynesia, America, Australia or Africa is hardly known to most British archaeologists or students. Most archaeologists, however, are anthropocentric (perhaps by definition?), though this is now being remedied by a greater awareness of the interdependence of humankind and other species; and of both and the natural environment. All archaeologists, however, who are not into SF are *terra*centric. The *Journal of Galactic Archaeology* has yet to reach its first issue, owing to the dismal failure of our astronauts or space probes to find living or dead civilizations on the moon or other planets. They can so far only be invented in SF.

115

## Modes of archaeological SF

The modes within which SF and archaeology have been or might be created may be listed as follows; they are of variable academic interest, or usefulness to archaeology:

(1) Terran archaeologists (that's us) investigating the remains of extinct civilizations on other worlds (or even the ethnography of living communities, of giant spiders with red eyes on stalks). These are very common in SF; even Captain Kirk occasionally included an archaeologist in his team chosen to beam down.

The academic point in such studies is to explore the extent to which archaeological method and theory are *universally* (*sic*) applicable to the study of material culture anywhere; or whether they are applicable only on earth, to the creations of *homo sapiens sapiens*. Biologists would certainly see the basic approaches of their discipline as applicable to any life-form, and so too should archaeologists. SF offer scope here for the development of abstract archaeological theory.

(2) Archaeologists from other worlds examining the remains of our (life-extinct) culture. This is much easier, because we are familiar with the material culture they will find. The interest here is in the extent to which objective archaeological approaches will get it all wrong. We have already seen a real-life example of this by Terran archaeologists (see Millie's Camp, pages 90–1). There are some excellent pieces in this genre. One of the most famous appeared in the *New Statesman* many years ago – an investigation of the ruins of the London Underground. This was entirely interpreted in ritual terms: the Line and Circle folk lived in this complex labyrinth with its rigid symbolism. At intervals there were special enclosed booths, in each of which was a ritual instrument linked by a wire to a special box, in which offerings could be made through slots.

One of Arthur Clarke's best stories concerns the reconstruction of hominid life on Earth based on a surviving artefact buried deeply in a time-capsule below fused concrete – a Walt Disney cartoon of Donald Duck. In David Lodge's *The British Museum is*

*Falling Down* (1965), it is suggested that the distribution of Roman Catholic households could be plotted by the incidence of broken thermometers used to determine the safe period for pious housewives. In a full-scale illustrated book, *The Motel of the Mysteries* (Macaulay, 1979), a motel room is found preserved intact, even with its door-hanger, 'Do not Disturb'. Inside are two skeletons. One lies on a ritual couch frozen in death while gazing at a glass-fronted box, which was apparently used to transmit messages to the faithful (not far out here!). Another skeleton was lying in a larger porcelain ritual receptacle, while close by was a smaller one with a hinged seat, and a long piece of paper in a roll on which to write one's thoughts. Reproductions of the latter receptacle in miniature were seen being sold on the site as souvenirs.

The point in all these is just the same as in Millie's Camp – what can we make of archaeological evidence if we don't know anything of the cultural background of the people whose remains we are studying? What are the *ways* in which we can get it wrong? This topic has recently been explored in relation to a body of evidence which had already been fully published in a conventional way (Rahtz and Watts, 1983). 'The Martian Expedition to Wharram Percy' (Phahtz, 1985) finds a series of stones close to a large non-domestic building. By analogy with others elsewhere which say 'Here Lies ...' (the Martians have been studying Earth for some time and know the basic framework of English), it is assumed that the stones cover burials, but nowhere is this explicit at Wharram – the purpose is clearly a memorial one. But the dead are there; Hon Jurst, the director of the expedition, has found Terran skeletons under the nearby building. Demographic data are worked out from information on the stones, with the assistance of a document dug up in the ruins of nearby *Eboracum* by the expedition's historian, Boris Meresford. The expedition, however, is defeated in trying to work out the religious beliefs of these Wharram Terrans. What is this place, Jesus, where someone goes to sleep? 'Heaven' seems to be a prize, awarded to those who do well. There are also quotations from one 'Mat', in archaic English of some centuries earlier. The author, Rilip Phahtz, had a serious purpose here: to determine what the stones really told us as artefacts, independently of what we knew about nineteenth- and twentieth-century culture and beliefs in England. This kind of study is 'distancing oneself from one's data', avoiding cultural bias in the observer.

(3) SF interpretations of archaeological evidence. This gets dangerously close to space fantasy, or the literary devices of historical novelists; and to the heresies put out by Von Däniken and his kind. An example here is Pierre Boulle's *Monkey Planet* (1966) in which future Terran archaeologists play a crucial role in showing that the planet had been occupied by humans before the great apes. In this category, too, come several stories of space-travellers landing on earth, surviving, degenerating and becoming the first hominids in our fossil record – an alternative creation myth.

(4) The reconstructions of a past which have an eye to the future. There has to be some hint, explicit or otherwise, that the past people being reconstructed are conscious of future students of their lifestyle, notably of archaeologists looking at their material culture. There is some suggestion of this in Angus Wilson's *Anglo-Saxon Attitudes* (1956) or in Golding's *The Inheritors* (1955). The idea is more explicit in the numerous jokes/cartoons about the deliberate 'fooling' of future archaeologists by creating patterns of artefacts that are not 'unconscious'. There is scope for much writing here, not only in the abstract, such as a scene where early people are depicted behaving in this way and talking about it, but where the actual finds of today (such as the Sutton Hoo ship-burial, or Stonehenge) are explained by reconstructions of elaborate past hoaxes (as the relics of Piltdown Man proved to be).

(5) Time-travel. Archaeologists who can travel in time and/or space clearly have a big advantage when it comes to cross-cultural, diachronic, or trans-spatial comparisons between different societies. Most of these restrict their travellers to Earth (except Dr Who; see also the end of the film *2001*), and rather sadly to contexts already partly known from history. Thus, the

tourist time-travellers in Silverberg's *Up the Line* (1969) want to go back to see historical events such as the Crucifixion or the sack of Constantinople. Because these are so popular, different couriers and their parties encounter each other in the milling crowds (the couriers even encounter *themselves* on successive visits). In another book in this genre (Kilworth, 1975), the crowd of time-travelling tourists help in the Crucifixion, thinking that they are thus blending in with the crowds of Jews and Romans; but in fact there isn't a crowd of Jews and Romans, there are only tourists.

Similarly Mark Twain's classic *A Connecticut Yankee at the Court of King Arthur* (1971/1889) is limited in its archaeological or historical appreciation of sixth-century England by a nineteenth-century American, but is a splendid essay in cross-cultural comparison. More imaginative is Robert Westall's *The Wind Eye* (1976), a children's classic in which a modern professor and his family sail into the mist off the Northumberland coast, and become involved in the world of St Cuthbert, lovingly delineated with an eye to archaeological and historical detail, and very evocative of the Farne Islands.

There is much room for new writing here in visiting older societies and seeing in the technology and material culture now being excavated parallels to our own world and checking our hypotheses; or even in the abstract concept of reversible time, where we are in fact encountering the future in order to predict the past (eh?).

(6) Archaeologists as part of intergalactic societies. Reconstructions of other societies sometimes include archaeologists, as in the first volume of Asimov's *Foundation* (1974), or in *The Hitch-Hiker's Guide to the Galaxy* (Adams, 1979). They serve as a useful device to SF writers to develop the *history* of other worlds.

## HISTORICAL NOVELS

There is obviously some overlap between these and the modes of SF listed above, notably number 4. The difference is perhaps only that in historical novels there is normally no introduction of the supernatural. If there is, it runs the danger of being condemned as a device unworthy of a great writer. Thus, Sir Walter Scott came under fire from contemporary critics for his inclusion in *The Monastery* of the White Lady of Avenel – a supernatural spirit who influences the action.

Many people find historical novels easier to read than straight history or archaeology books, because the form allows the fleshing out of the rather sparse facts with a wealth of detail and dialogue, and some insight into what characters are thinking and feeling. The more historically plausible such detail is, the better the book. Scott's masterpieces concerning Ivanhoe, Kenilworth, Rob Roy, the Civil War or 'the '45' are so convincing that one has to be alert to the truth that it is fiction one is reading. Many people owe their total knowledge of the French Revolution to *A Tale of Two Cities*, or of the Roman emperors to Robert Graves' *I, Claudius* (the latter is also full of splendid archaeological detail).

In historical novels proper, the imaginative reconstruction of the past is much easier, as written sources give the writer a good start in anything about the last two thousand years; and once again, *named people* are crucial to the maintenance of the reader's interest. With more remote periods, the task is more difficult, and much more open to criticism: principally because the authors have not troubled to find out about the archaeology, and so the framework is hopelessly implausible, as in the film *A Million Years BC* where hominids co-exist with dinosaurs and pterodactyls. Others are, however, excellent and show evidence of considerable research, as in the *Asterix* series.

One of the most remarkable achievements in this genre is Jean Auel's series. *The Clan of the Cave Bear, The Valley of the Horses, The Mammoth Hunters* and *The Plains of Passage* (Auel 1980, 1982, 1986, 1990). These take a very remote period and area – the Upper Palaeolithic of about 35,000 BC in the Caspian area of Eastern Europe. The story's heroine is Ayla. She is of *Homo sapiens sapiens* stock, but as a young child she is orphaned by an earthquake. She is picked up by a travelling band of quite different people, of Neanderthal type (*Homo Neanderthalis*). They take her back to their cave, a large one accommodating a whole kin-group. She is here brought up in their cultural traditions, including the bear cult of the first title; although she is to them something of a freak, and rather 'ugly' with her high forehead, fair hair, stance and (oddly) her ability to cry, she does in fact provoke some enmity. When adolescent she is mated to a rather unpleasant young man. Sex is male-orientated in this society, and hardly more than sanctioned rape in the animal posture, its biological purpose not understood. Apart from this, the Neanderthals are sympathetically portrayed as a sensitive people of rich culture, especially knowledgeable about medicine from herbs, and in balance with the environment.

The group in the cave is aware that 'far away' to the north there are people like Ayla, whom they have occasionally encountered on hunting expeditions. By the time she is 14, her position becomes untenable; she sets off to find her people, perforce leaving her child behind. After some arduous travels, during which she learns survival techniques, she meets one of her own kind, a handsome young man (an all-American hero, as the author writes in the USA) named Jondalar; she saves him from death by a lion that answers to her call – she tamed it as a cub. She has also, to Jondalar's amazement, learned to tame and ride a horse – a thing he's never heard of. They do of course fall in love, to the accompaniment of purple passages (which were presumably designed to sell the books) and copulate in the 'missionary position' (I don't *think* there is any archaeological evidence for this cultural divide!).

They eventually meet up with a major group of *Hom. sap. sap.* who are living in houses and have a rather more advanced technology. Although under Jondalar's protection, Ayla is the subject of some contumely when it is disclosed that she has lived with, and been mated within, a group of people who are generally regarded as inferior and hardly better than animals (compare page 33). Ayla is horrified, because she has a great affection for many of the Neanderthal group she lived with, who saved her life, cared for her and initiated her into their mysteries and learning. The *Hom. sap. sap.* are, however, very impressed by her horse-riding ability, and things improve.

One feels that if she'd stayed around, she would eventually

have invented traffic lights in the camp; but in the fourth book she and Jondalar ride into the sunset, to set off on a long journey to the area where his family live, in the Dordogne.

Described baldly and in such brevity, this all sounds ridiculous. It is not, however; in the three thousand pages so far published the human actions are played out against a spendidly portrayed landscape, climate, fauna and flora (and as far as I know reasonably interpreted); and what little is known about the culture and technology of the two major hominid species is delineated with skill. To get all this approximately right, Jean Auel talked to many archaeologists and anthropologists, read all she could on this period and area, visited museums, and drew on her own considerable cultural background in America, notably concerning the American Indian use of herbs and other natural healing materials. Each volume is even prefaced by a map with illustrations of Upper Palaeolithic figurines.

Apart from being absorbingly good reading, the books seem to me to be highly convincing as a picture of the mode of life of two very diverse human communities in the post-glacial period in the Caspian. Leaving aside the human loves and hates, I felt I understood more of what life was really like for the users of the lithic assemblages which are most of what survive to us; and that the books merit the status of a major complex hypothesis which archaeologists could take seriously and comment on. I fear that my colleagues in Upper Palaeolithic archaeology will not, however, do this – it is doubtful whether they will even read it, or regard it as anything but sub-literary rubbish. No such inhibitions need though deter the readers of this book, to whom Jean Auel is highly recommended.

### THE PURSUIT OF TRUTH

We have seen in chapters 2 and 3 that the academic and high-minded pursuit of the truth about the past is not the mainspring of motivation for most archaeology. The desire for truth is not by any means universal, even if the concept of truth, or even the truth about any particular topic, *could* be universal. This is just as well, as disputes about the 'facts' of the past in archaeology or history, and their interpretation, provide the principal material for scholarly debate. Even so, among academics there is a general agreement that the common aim is to get as near as possible to finding out what did happen in the past, and why it happened, even if the latter was not at all clear to the people to whom things were happening.

For many people, the facts about the past are not of any great interest. They are concerned more with how the image conjured up by history or archaeology can be used in their own imagination, or even perverted to support theories. Leaving on one side most of the non-academic motives for archaeology listed in chapters 2 and 3, such as its use for political manipulation, we now concentrate on two: the use of archaeology to support religious belief, and its use to support myth. It may be difficult to disentangle these two: one person's religion is another person's myth.

Here I want to concentrate on the apparent dislike of scientific truth or at best the inability to decide what is scientific. This is a turning away from rationalism and from basic concepts of logic. Although most of my examples will be semi-humorous (because to laugh at anything is often the best mode of attack – my text is really derision), I do find the lunatic fringe of archaeology highly distasteful. Distortion of the truth or even the suppression of it is the antithesis of all I believe in, and directly counter to my own aims as an archaeologist. The lunatic fringe may seem to be harmless eccentrics, but to me they are as potentially dangerous to human society (even if they have the best intentions) as the other perverters of truth, the tyrants and dictators. I will first examine the reasons why some people like irrational things related to archaeology, and then illustrate this with examples, drawn from a vast field. In the final section I will give a case-study of Glastonbury. Here I can speak with some authority, as I dug there for six seasons.

## The magnetism of the irrational

Certain people reject scientific truth for several reasons:
   1   A dislike of science, logic, and reason, because they are

associated with scientific, logical and reasonable people, whom our group 1 find irritating and inhuman, lacking 'normal' passions and emotion; notably schoolmasters, scientists, statisticians and others in authority. These make our group 1 feel inferior and ignorant, because they find it difficult to see the difference between common sense (which 'must be true' because it is rooted in everyday experience) and anything which is not easily understood.

2   An attraction towards the mystic, hidden 'real' truths, not accessible to those who need proof or a reasoned argument. Truths of this kind are, it is claimed, known intuitively to poets, artists, saints, gurus, mystics, drug-addicts and 'primitive people'. Such knowledge was, in this argument, formerly part of the common heritage, but it has been 'lost' in the development of civilization, and can only be recovered in non-scientific ways.

3   A belief that science and reason are actually evil, in that they are often opposed to religious belief, which is based on faith, not reason (though many great scientists and other scholars seem to manage to live in both worlds). The Oxford Laboratory recently received a letter accusing them of promoting evil in that they were, in their new radiocarbon dating work, seeking to overthrow the word of God, as represented in a literal interpretation of the Bible. Evangelical Christians the world over are seeking to discredit radiocarbon dating, especially when, as in Australia, it supported an antiquity of 40,000 years for the 'inferior' Aborigines (chapter 2), though in the next breath they will be claimed as a relic of the time before people were made in the divine image.

4   A liking for the romantic, which is believed to be more interesting and exciting than bare historical truth. If King Arthur didn't actually exist, he should have done. Archaeologists and historians who discredit Arthur, or the story of Alfred burning the cakes, or rape-and-pillage Vikings, are 'spoilers', depriving the common people of their cultural heritage. Exotic explanations are more palatable than boring archaeological ones. The prime evidence for this is the colossal sales of Von Däniken's books, and the rather more respectable sagas of Thor Heyerdahl.

Von Däniken sought to show, among other things, that many of the most striking monuments of the past had been built with the help of earlier spacemen. A South American relief sculpture was interpreted as a representation of such an extraterrestial visitor, looking very much like an American astronaut, complete with space-suit and bubble hat. To the eternal credit of the BBC they devoted a two-hour programme to a detailed exposé not only of Von Däniken's failure to observe elementary laws of evidence and logic, but also to his having resorted to suppression or downright fraud to bolster up his fantasy. The sad thing was, as the BBC hammered home, that far from restoring to the people their lost knowledge, their true cultural heritage, he was in fact depriving them of it, by denying to people the great achievements of art and great stone monuments which their ancestors created without the help of God or spacemen. He was denigrating human beings.

5 Irrationality provides a free-for-all platform. Since there are no rules, anyone can win. The 'expert' is no longer top dog ('experts baffled' is a favourite among journalists). Who can gainsay that anything is possible, or that two or three coincidences make a fact? Everyone can be his or her own savant, and nobody need feel inferior any more – you don't have to have a university education to arrive at intuitive proofs.

### Ley lines

Ley lines are courses or paths of earth energy. They are marked by ancient features; if several of these line up on a map, this is likely to be a ley line. It is believed by ley-liners that these paths were known to Neolithic people, who could store their energy in henge-monuments. As with other ancient knowledge, these skills were, it is claimed, later lost. The points chosen need not be all of the same date or type – a line can run through a tree, or a church, or an old burial mound; the idea is that there is a continuity in time of those spots being utilized.

The argument for and against ley lines were sympathetically examined by Tom Williamson and Liz Bellamy (1983), who concluded that there was no evidence that they ever existed.

## Dowsing or divining

These are much more respectable techniques. Diviners, using a variety of similar devices such as wands or forked sticks of wood, plastic or metal, can and do find water, water-pipes, metals and other buried things. There may well be a scientific explanation for the slight reaction of the human body to buried features, which makes itself manifest by a muscular twitch which causes the apparatus to move vertically or horizontally. While this cannot yet be demonstrated scientifically, it does work. Farmers and oil companies pay diviners money to seek the presence of oil or water. A recent academic study in Northumberland has made a strong case for the ability of an experienced diviner to recover the plans of long-vanished walls of early churches (Bailey et al., 1988). Dowsing on the ground may be acceptable; what the rationalist finds harder to swallow is divining on *maps*, which is clearly moving towards the paranormal world of psychic phenomena. The diviner may well be a useful adjunct to the archaeologist's battery of ground-sensing devices (as is the metal detector in the right hands). Dowsing can, however, lead to pure fantasy of the most dangerous kind.

## America's past

We have already mentioned, in chapter 2, the varied motivations of American archaeology, one of which is the search for the archaeologists' roots. In the lunatic fringe here much effort is expended in proving the case for non-indigenous, pre-Columbus visits or even colonizations, by Phoenicians, refugees from drowned Atlantis, the lost tribes of Israel, New England Celts, ancient astronauts, Vikings and Prince Madoc the Welshman.

Fantastic claims are made for patently faked archaeological finds such as the Kensington 'rune-stone', and the Vinland map (Davies, 1979; see also a series of witty exposés by Glyn Daniel in many issues of *Antiquity*.)

Commercial interests capitalize on public credulity. In North Salem, New Hampshire, there is a site called Mystery Hill, 'America's Stonehenge – 2000 BC'. This is a 20-ha complex of stone buildings, walls, wells, drains and other features, including a 4½-tonne granite slab on stone legs. The structures have been attributed variously to Irish Culdee monks about AD 1000, to 'megalithic' immigrants of about 2000 BC, or (probably more realistically) to Jonathan Pattee between 1832 and 1849. Archaeoastronomy is also dragged in: 'it can now be stated that Mystery Hill is, among other things, unquestionably a calendrical site able to determine solar and lunar movements with utmost accuracy.' ... 'slabs with strange markings' ... 'translated as being of ancient European Scripts' ... 'more work must be done ... before the inscriptions will be accepted by the academic community.' All this falls hardly short of fraud, and should be discouraged by the USA tourist authorities. It is an insult to the American public, to the indigenous Indian and to Pattee.

*Other wonders*

One of the most persistent quests in archaeology is the search for Noah's Ark on Mount Ararat in Turkey. The Secretary of the General Council of Seventh-day Adventists said in 1964 that he was convinced that pieces of wood brought down from 14,000 feet up on the mountain were part of a giant boat (two-thirds of the size of the *Queen Mary*). There were several hundreds of tons of wood under an ice pack; the timber was tooled and it was a type of oak so hard that electrical blades had been broken in cutting it. In 1965 the *Daily Telegraph* published an air-photograph of another ark on Ararat, 400 feet long. Geologists, however, dismissed the shape as having been caused by erosion of volcanic rocks about a million years ago.

In England, there have been problems about the use of Stonehenge at the time of the midsummer solstice; two groups claim rights to use the monument for their activities. The first are the latterday druids, who assert a link with their pre-Roman forebears. The second are a larger contingent of pop-festival participants; they believe that Stonehenge has a special relevance for such modern folk-gatherings.

Unfortunately their camps and activities pose a threat to the integrity of the monument, and their rubbish and cesspits disturb the archaeologically very rich surrounding area. All this has led to confrontation with land-owners, English Heritage and ultimately the police; and there has been some violence and oppression. The problems pose the question 'Who owns Stonehenge?', and the reader will find a series of views on both sides in a book of the same title (Chippindale, 1989).

Many more examples could be quoted of the world of alternative archaeology, but all pale before the Mecca of all irrationality: the sacred Isle of Avalon, Glastonbury, to which we will now turn for a detailed case-study.

## Glastonbury

The present small town of Glastonbury in Somerset is part of a promontory which protrudes into the low-lying and marshy areas of the Somerset Levels, extending to the Bristol Channel. Although there is a neck of land above flooding level connecting Glastonbury to higher ground to the east, its appearance as an 'island' is accentuated by a striking steep hill over 150 metres high. This is Glastonbury Tor, a prominent landmark which can be seen from up to 30 km away. The area is rich in archaeology. As early as the fifth millennium BC there were early Neolithic settlements in the Levels, on small drier areas, linked by well-carpentered wooden trackways, found excellently preserved in the peat, with many artefacts of the same period. Many further trackways of later millennia have been excavated, and in the centuries just before Christ there were marsh-edge settlements here, well known as the 'Glastonbury and Meare Lake Villages', one of the richest, best preserved and most extensively excavated archaeological sites in Britain. There are many finds at Glastonbury itself of Roman date, indicating the presence of a villa on the lower ground.

In my excavations on the summit of the Tor, I found wooden buildings and finds of the sixth century AD, including pieces of pottery from the Eastern Mediterranean (see chapter 3 for some discussion of these). The site might have been the stronghold of a Dark Age chieftain, or an early monastic site.

In the later seventh or early eighth century, a monastery with an important church was founded on the lower ground and received much support from the Anglo-Saxon kings of Wessex and England. Dunstan was its abbot in the tenth century. Several satellite monasteries were established in the eighth or ninth centuries; these included one on the Tor, of which I excavated what may have been the timber church and a few rock-cut cells. Another was at Beckery, on the edge of the marshes, where I excavated the whole church and cemetery (Rahtz and Hirst, 1974).

In the Middle Ages, Glastonbury flourished. A church of St Michael was built on the Tor, whose tower crowns it to this day. The Norman and later abbey was one of the richest in the land. Its abbot, Richard Whiting, was hanged on the Tor by Henry VIII's officials at the Dissolution in the sixteenth century, it is said for refusing to reveal the whereabouts of the abbey treasure.

After the Dissolution, Glastonbury declined. The abbey was destroyed and most of its stone was carted away, leaving only some still impressive ruins today. The site was acquired by the Church of England in the earlier part of this century (to the annoyance of the Roman Catholic Church, which has course a much better claim to it), and there are now annual Christian festivals, pilgrimages and other events.

One might think that all this archaeology and history was exciting enough to stir anyone's imagination. Glastonbury has, however, during the last fifty years, but especially since the 1960s, become the magnet for an incredible variety of hippies, weirdos, drop-outs and psychos, of every conceivable belief and in every stage of dress and undress, flowing hair and uncleanliness. How has this come about? We may point to several reasons. The striking natural topography and the long religious associations have attracted those who seek enlightenment in a Christian context. The main lure has been some 'alternative archaeology' of the distant past. The medieval monks, in their efforts to make Glastonbury an important centre of pilgrimage and to attract wealth, made extravagant claims about the antiquity of the abbey. They produced documents which purported to show that Joseph of Arimathea had come to Glastonbury after the death of Christ, and had brought with him phials containing the blood and sweat of Jesus. William of Malmesbury, writing in the twelfth century, records what the monks told him, though he may have been sceptical as to their truth. They also, at the end of the twelfth century, claimed to have disinterred the body of none other than King Arthur, in a deep grave, in a dug-out coffin. With him was a lead cross on which was inscribed HIC IACET SEPULTUS INCLITUS REX ARTURIUS IN INSULA AVALONIA (Here lies buried the famous King Arthur in the Island of Avalon.) This lead cross that they claimed to have found survived to be drawn and published in the seventeenth century. Modern academic opinion, but by no means unanimously, believes that the whole of the documentary evidence, and that of the grave, was a total monkish invention with no basis in fact.

From the twelfth century to the present day the Glastonbury legends grew. Guinevere with long yellow hair had joined Arthur in his grave. The visitors to Glastonbury now included not only Joseph, but also Jesus Christ, brought as a boy by Joseph on an earlier trip to get tin; party of his schooldays were spent at the druidic college at Glastonbury, where the best education in the world could be obtained. To these were added Mary the mother of Jesus, and even Mary Magdalene. The accretion of legends have become fact in the minds of the Avalonians. The Chalice Well is still believed to be the place where Joseph deposited the phials (though my excavations there proved the 'well' to be a medieval well-house, built around a spring to safeguard the water supply to the abbey, and gradually buried in silt: Rahtz, 1964). A flowering thorn bush on a nearby hill called Wirral was Joseph's staff planted when he arrived, crying out (in English) to his party (to explain the name) 'Friends, we are weary all.' Another story of course has Joseph bringing the Holy Grail, a wooden cup. King Arthur's grave is still shown to visitors in the grounds of the abbey.

This is not all, however. One of the most remarkable claims about the area in the 1930s was that the hills around bore the signs of the zodiac. These were outlined by hedgelines, banks, roads, lanes, tracks and any other lines that could be invoked (rather like the ley lines discussed above). They could be traced out on maps and on air-photographs, and were published in full by the late Katherine Maltwood (1935, 1937). The zodiac still has many supporters, but the fallacious basis of the evidence on which it was delineated was discussed in a dispassionate and scientific way by Ian Burrow (1983).

The Tor itself has attracted its share of legends. Two ideas that still persist in Glastonbury are (a) that it is an artificial mound, and (b) that it is hollow inside. A more credible theory was put forward by the late Geoffrey Russell, and taken up and elaborated by Geoffrey Ashe (1979), who lives at its foot. This is that the Tor is a kind of three dimensional maze, of which the 'paths' are formed by an arrangement of terraces around its steep slopes. The pattern postulated – a widespread symbol – is similar to many other mazes such as those on the floor of Charters Cathedral, on Cretan coins, on a pillar at Pompeii etc. The conventional explanation of the terraces is that they are natural (the result of the differential erosion of the varying strata of which the Tor is made) or that they are strip lynchets (for medieval agriculture). I am sufficiently open-minded on this one to have said in print, 'The argument is complex, but is worth consideration ... if the maze theory were demonstrated to be true, it would clearly be of the greatest relevance to the origins of Glastonbury as a centre.' I would still stick to this. Such technology as the 'sculpting' of a hill would not be in any way beyond the capacity of Neolithic man, who we know was settled in the area; and the models made by Geoffrey Russell do look quite convincing.

The Tor is also a centre of witchcraft. I was visited on my dig there by an exotic lady who claimed to be the 'white' witches' queen. We had an interesting conversation, during the course of which she told me, among other things, that we were digging in the wrong place (?). We found rather unpleasant evidence of witchcraft practices beneath the church tower, and had a nasty experience with a 'black' hypnotist on the Tor.

In the light of all this, it is hardly surprising that Glastonbury attracted very large numbers of young people in the 1960s in the world-wide movement concerned with seeking new values in an evil world, a movement that had its origins in America and spread through Europe to Katmandu and the Far East. The Love

People and Flower Power are part of social history now, but their impact on Glastonbury in 1969 was immense. Something of this was expressed in words which I cannot hope to emulate, by Jon Pepper (*The Guardian*, 20 December 1969); I quote from his article:

'The Hippie Vale of Avalon'
The frosts and fogs have come to Avalon. The deep, brooding mysteries still cling to the vale, even more so in the present melds of haze and wintry sunbeams, but the 1969 Children's Crusades to Glastonbury in search of the town's strange enchantments have finally ended, defeated by the cold. The fields are now empty of their tents and flutes. The place has sunk into a thankful hibernation.... Predictably, however, while the tents of the new visitors have dotted the hillsides, they have crossed the townspeople.

The arrival of the pilgrims – and the cult of Glastonbury which now looks well set among the Love people – has led to paroxysms of righteous horror from some of the town elders, particularly the trustees of the Chalice Well, whose holy, healing waters have apparently been used for communal ablutions. Of course, the intruders cannot do anything right: half the town acusses them of being unwashed and an affront to civilisation, while the other half berates them for washing their jeans, shaving and sprucing up in the Chalice Well Waters.... For the young Utopians, however, Glastonbury, as one devotee has written, is strong magic. Muz Murray told me: 'It's my contention that the Tor and the giant zodiac imprinted on the landscape round Glastonbury, which has had enough written about it now to hold some veracity, were together the centre of cosmic power in Atlantean days.' ... Clearly, Glastonbury is crying out for deep examination. A group of academics and writers calling itself the Research into Lost Knowledge Organisation are now trying to do just this. So far they have produced learned but empty-ended reports. Full aerial reconnaissance of Glastonbury, archaeological excavations of the Tor, and a massive concentration of cooperative intellectual effort from the appropriate university departments aimed at sorting out the real wood from the trees ought to be undertaken!

The sad thing about this is his plea for archaeological excavations on the Tor: I *did* excavate the summit in between 1964 and 1966 (Rahtz, 1971), but clearly our (quite epic) effort remained unnoticed, even so soon after as three years.

Glastonbury still has many visitors, and inspires visions in people. One lady came to see me from California. Although she had no previous background knowledge of Glastonbury or its legends, she had a series of visions of underground chambers in one of the Glastonbury hills. These were very clear and explicit, 'just like a coloured movie', she later told me. She was so disturbed and obsessed by them, and her husband got so worried about her, that they spent all their savings (14,000 dollars – they were not very wealthy people) to come to Glastonbury. They had heard of my work in Somerset, and came to see me first where I was then digging. There was no doubt whatsoever of her sincerity. She produced a series of drawings, done from memory, which were very detailed about what would be found in the underground chamber. I set her on the road to Glastonbury, and although she had never been to England before, she unhesitatingly identified Wirral Hill as the scene of her vision, and pointed out where excavation would locate the chamber. She was naturally very disappointed that archaeological resources were not available to test the truth of her vision, but she returned to America satisfied at least that she had seen the right spot. The experience she related is by no means unique, but the only one of which I have had first-hand experience.

Finally in this study of Glastonbury we may look at the history of excavations there, which are quite a saga in themselves. The first excavations were in the abbey grounds, in the shadow of the great ruinous fragments of the complex of churches. This was in the years following the acquisition of the site by the Church. Two or three directors were involved in the work, which was not of very good quality, and was never fully published. The last of them in this first campaign was a remarkable figure, Frederick

133

Bligh Bond, an architect and mystic. Like many others at that time and since, he believed that the abbey site was the earliest Christian nucleus in Britain, already the seat of a druidic college in prehistoric times. As one of the Glastonbury faithful said to me, 'Christianity was already present at Glastonbury in the first century BC; it was only waiting for Christ's birth to be given its name.' Bond accordingly looked for evidence that would prove these earliest associations, including (as he believed) the plan of a circular monastery (a church in the middle, and cells round the edge of the circle). In his search for this and other important early features, he claimed to have had guidance by spirit writing from a medieval monk of Glastonbury, who told him exactly where to dig. Not surprisingly, the Church disapproved of his unethical approach, and in 1921 closed the excavations down precipitately, to quote Bond, 'without warning and before my measurements could be taken'. Bond retired to America.

My own involvement began in 1962 at the invitation of the Chalice Well Trust, and its Chairman, W. Tudor Pole; he was a remarkable man, another mystic, who believed in reincarnation. He himself could, he told me, remember three previous existences. The first was in the first century AD, when he was present at the important events in Jerusalem. The second was in the seventh century, when he worked in the library of the Great Palace of Constantinople. He once showed me a list of all the books there, which he claimed to have remembered. He in fact took part in the excavations there in the 1930s, perhaps hoping the library would be found. The third existence was as a cardinal in the fourteenth century AD. He is well known for his books on spiritualism and especially for the book he wrote jointly with the famous novelist Rosamund Lehmann, concerning her daughter Sally, who had died young in tragic circumstances.

Tudor Pole understood archaeology, but clearly hoped that I too would find evidence to support the early legends. I was commissioned first to dig at the Chalice Well, with the results I have mentioned above. Then there were my three seasons at the Tor, and later two at Beckery Chapel. Though the archaeological results were of the greatest interest, I had not perhaps found what was hoped for. Tudor Pole never expressed dissatisfaction or disappointment – he knew I was finding all that was there – but some of his disciples were not so complimentary. One said, 'Mr Rahtz, I can give you three reasons why you haven't found anything: (1) You're digging in the wrong place' (in this she agreed with the witches' Queen); '(2) You're digging at the wrong time'(?); and '(3) you're the wrong person' – I really couldn't win!

Glastonbury illustrates the enormous gulfs that separate the aims, methods and expectations of the scientific archaeologist from those who seek lost knowledge. Is the gulf as wide between the archaeologist and the general public? In my last chapter (9) we shall look at this public, and ask what archaeology means or could mean to them.

# 8

# Two Case-Studies in British Archaeology

These two studies, Sutton Hoo and Wharram Percy, have been chosen because they are both well known outside Britain, have a long background history, are highly significant in their own field, but are different from each other in almost every other respect. They illustrate many of the concepts and problems that this book has dealt with.

## SUTTON HOO

### Earlier work

This is a cemetery of burial mounds on a terrace at the edge of cultivated land overlooking the estuary of the River Deben in Suffolk. Although there is prehistoric occupation on the site, the fame of the place lies in its Anglo-Saxon connections. It is believed to be one of the burial places, if not the principal or only one, of the kings of the dynasty which ruled East Anglia in the sixth–seventh centuries AD. This claim rests partly on a number of isolated finds from robbed-out mounds, but principally on the results of a remarkable excavation which took place there in 1939. The then owner, Mrs E.M. Pretty, decided, partly at least from active curiosity, that she would like the barrows on her

136

land opened. She entrusted the work to Ipswich Museum, and they to an archaeologist of some local reputation, Basil Brown. In 1938 he partly excavated three mounds with only minor results. In the fourth, opened in 1939, he very soon came across the remains of a ship, of which only corroded clench nails, soil discolorations and textural differences in sand were still present. The uncovering and photography of this ghost of a ship in 1939 was quite a *tour de force*. Brown quickly realized that it was a burial-ship, which had not been robbed in antiquity.

News of the discovery got to the then Office of Works, who invited Charles Phillips to take over. He organized a small team of the leading archaeologists of the day, and they assembled on the site at very short notice. It was August 1939, and war was only a month away.

The burial deposit was immensely rich and important; it was worth many millions of pounds, and its bequest by Mrs Pretty to the nation one of the largest such gifts ever made. It is remarkable, looking back from half a century on, that usable records were made at all. The team did not even have an excavation hut, and the astonishing finds of gold, silver and many other materials were packed for despatch to the British Museum in moss. Once the richness of the deposit was realized, strict security had to be maintained.

All was safely stored away by the time war broke out. It was many years before the British Museum could begin the work of conservation and publication. Between the fifties and the seventies this was entrusted to Rupert Bruce-Mitford, who has now published three great volumes on the ship-burial (Bruce-Mitford, 1975–83). He also directed a re-excavation of the mound in 1963–71, to clear up outstanding problems and to take a plaster cast of the boat.

Although no actual body was found, probably because of the acid conditions, the mound is generally believed to have been the burial place of King Redwald, who died *c*.625, a man of power and fame in his day. Readers who have not seen the Sutton Hoo finds should without delay visit the British Museum, where they are splendidly displayed (Evans, 1986).

*The new initiative*

My case-study is not, however, about the 1939 excavation and its long aftermath, but about the new excavations which are now in their final stages. I shall look at the long process of planning that brought this new initiative to fruit; the legal, financial, academic, personality and other problems that had to be overcome; the structure of the sponsoring and controlling organizations; the aims of the work; the new methods being used; and the preliminary results up to the time this book goes to press. This background should prepare readers for a proper appreciation of work that has been taking place there, and its exposition by the BBC among others. Nothing could be more different in aims, organization and method than the 1939 excavation and the present campaign.

The successive publications of the ship-burial had already inspired a great deal of learned comment from archaeologists and historians, especially those in Britain, Scandinavia and Germany. Many new problems were posed, many new questions were asked. It was generally agreed that many of the problems raised could be answered by further work in the field. A lot was known about one mound, and a very little about three others, but virtually nothing of the cemetery as a whole, or its immediate area, or its regional context within East Anglia. Many believed that further digging should be done, but there was also a big faction who were against it, for reasons discussed below.

Rupert Bruce-Mitford was, however, convinced that further excavation and field-work were matters of high priority in British archaeology generally, and he approached me to discuss ways in which we might further the project. We formed a small steering committee, which included Rosemary Cramp, Barry Cunliffe and the late Robert Pretty, the son of the 1939 owner; he had retained the 'archaeological rights' in the land, and also wanted to see more work done.

Now began an uphill battle which took four years to win, and which generated for me alone three box-files full of paper. Discretion precludes a frank and honest exposé of the details of the saga, though the papers will be excellent material for the historians of archaeology and of archaeologists in the next century! Suffice it to say here there were many problems connected with personalities and institutions: this is nothing new in archaeology.

First there was funding and sponsorship. It was generally agreed that the British Museum with its great resources and expertise should be a major sponsor. The Society of Antiquaries also wished to support a major new research project. In the end, our small steering committee was absorbed into a joint committee of the SOA and BM, with generous support from the National Maritime Museum (which was interested in further data on boats), the BBC (which saw here the material for a splendid TV series) and the Suffolk County Council. Their archaeologists, notably Stanley West and Keith Wade, had for some time been working on the wider problems of the area, and their participation was essential. Two committees now control the project – a small executive committee deals with the action needed, and a larger, more representative one which meets once a year to hear and comment on reports of results.

By no means everybody agreed, however, that *any* work should go ahead. Many objectors were vociferous in their opposition.

### The great debate

The debate may be summarized by listing the arguments put forward by those opposed to the work, followed in each case by our response.

*Objection A*   The site is a safe one, not subject to the hazards of ploughing, or of motorway, quarrying or other development; it has a measure of legal protection. Excavation is by definition *destruction* of the monument. It is the duty of this generation to preserve monuments, and the archaeology contained within them, not to destroy them. The longer Sutton Hoo is left, the better. Each successive generation uses better techniques and recovers more data than its predecessors. We are trustees for those that come after. Unlike endangered species, historic sites cannot reproduce themselves; each one is unique. The site should be given extra legal and physical protection. (This is the familiar 'rescue versus research' debate: Rahtz, 1974.)

*Answer* The site is not safe. Rabbits, moles and bracken are destroying underground evidence. Two-legged predators armed with metal detectors are rife in the area. Ploughing was encroaching on the edges of the protected area. A large hole was dug in the centre of one of the shallow, unexcavated barrows to a depth of over a metre, into the subsoil, by persons unknown.

While it is true that each generation does better and better archaeology, what is the point of preserving data if they are *never* to be realized? Who will decide when the time has come? Each generation has a right to dig at least *part* of such a crucial site. Excavation is not destruction of the *monument*; any mound can and will be restored to its former appearance after excavation. The monument will be much more interesting and educational because of the extra understanding that archaeology has provided. How are techniques to be improved if not through prestige projects like this one? One of the avowed aims of the work has always been to use Sutton Hoo as a 'test-bed' for new techniques of prediction, excavation, recording and analysis.

*Objection B* Sutton Hoo is exotic and unique. While this makes it attractive to museum sponsors or the BBC, it is not really in the mainstream of British archaeology, which should be concerned with the broader patterns of ordinary human settlement, not with the burial-places of kings. The resources put into Sutton Hoo (about a million pounds over ten years) could more profitably be deployed in a dozen other equally worthwhile but less exotic Anglo-Saxon projects. Publicity given to the Sutton Hoo project will encourage the mistaken belief that archaeologists dig for treasure not knowledge.

*Answer* While exotic and unique sites are not ones on which to base general theories of settlement development, they are an important part of it. A case can be made academically for understanding as much as possible about the highest level of Anglo-Saxon society, its barrows and other burial places; such problems can be answered *only* by excavations of this kind. The massive amount of scholarly writing generated by the 1939 discoveries is witness to widespread academic interest in this kind of archaeology, in this country and abroad. There is a need to expand the 1939 database, and to put its content into a wider context, both in relation to the cemetery itself, and in its local and regional setting. The resources available for Sutton Hoo will *not* be available for any other project, being private research money; only a site like Sutton Hoo could attract such funds in sufficient quantity.

It is to the advantage of archaeology as a whole that public interest in the past *is* stimulated, and how better than by excavating a site that is already famous? Mounting a controlled scientific expedition at a site where public expectations are of glamorous finds and treasure is the best way of educating people to the real meaning of archaeology. It is easier to put over modern archaeology to a public that is 'captive' and already excited (even if initially for the wrong reasons). In Sutton Hoo there is uniquely a coincidence of academic and popular interest. Through the BBC, site tours, the local (Woodbridge) museum, and other ways, it will be possible gradually to replace the excitement already present in the public at the prospect of treasure by the alternative excitement of the understanding of Anglo-Saxon culture, archaeological method and complex explanation, all carried out in a highly professional and responsible way.

*Objection C* Whatever the sponsors may say about their high-minded and academic approach, their motives are suspect; they are really after more 'loot' like that found in 1939. The project is elitist in conception. There has been no full and open discussion either of the aims of the project, or of the methods appropriate to its execution.

*Answer* 'Loot' is not the primary objective of the project, though further finds of high quality would undoubtedly help to put the 1939 objects into a better context. Understanding the cemetery as a whole, and its immediate surroundings, is the primary aim. There has been extensive publicity of the project; a session was specially arranged at the Anglo-Saxon Cemeteries Conference at Oxford on Sutton Hoo, where I set out the pros and cons (Rahtz, 1979b). An important feature of the work is extensive field-work in the area, with the collaboration of the Suffolk County Council, to find out as much as possible of the whole Anglo-Saxon settlement pattern. Finally, the site has been made safe, and as much as possible found out about the site as a whole by every known prospecting device.

## Legal problems

The reader may wonder why, if the project is to be funded by private money, there has to be so much time and effort (and space in these pages) devoted to answering the arguments of objectors whose money is not being spent as would be the case if this were a publicly sponsored and financed excavation.

The reason is that Sutton Hoo is a scheduled site, protected by law. While it is difficult for legal protection to be enforced against rabbits or human burrowings (or even an airport or motorway, if such were to be planned to cross the area), it can be invoked to prohibit even scientific and highly respectable excavations. Under recent legislation, applications for consent to excavate a scheduled site will be given only if there is 'no serious objection from informed academic opinion', and if the proposed work is 'in the public interest'. In the case of Sutton Hoo, academic opinion was clearly not unanimous. Objectors can force a public enquiry.

## Current work

The new director of the work is Martin Carver. He is an ex-military man, like other great archaeologists before him (including Mortimer Wheeler). Like myself, he entered archaeology late. In his case this was through a graduate course at Durham. He made a name for himself by his work in urban archaeology, making substantial and imaginative contributions, by excavation and writing, to Durham, Lichfield, Stafford, Worcester and Shrewsbury. He has also been successful in integrating a field unit into the archaeology course at the University of Birmingham; and he is now Professor of Archaeology at York.

His initial task was to prepare a research design. This comprised a detailed proposal of the aims of the project, the programme of work planned, the timing of each phase and a detailed costing. Such documents, while common enough in commerce and industry, are still rare in archaeology, but management skills like this are increasingly important and should form parts of all archaeologists' training. Carver defined a research design, which sets out the background to the work of the project:

> Although a further harvest of valuable objects is not anticipated (and does not form any part of these objectives), the burial assemblage from mound 1 has undoubtedly won, by its beauty and vivacity, many new friends for archaeology through its display in the British Museum. It is perverse to disdain objects which are universally admired; such admiration should rather be transformed into understanding, and this the project aims to do.

The regional survey is left in the hands of the County Council, through its field archaeologists West and Wade, in close association with Carver. But the principal expenditure of resources has been on the site itself, and its immediate locality of the Deben estuary. Carver's strategy here is divided into two parts: *evaluation* and *excavation*; these are accompanied by campaigns connected with site management, publicity and education, and the regional study of the Sutton Hoo area and the Anglo-Saxon kingdom of East Anglia. Martin Carver has been active in travelling round the country, seeking commercial and academic help in cash and in kind. A series of academic seminars has also been held at the universities of Cambridge, East Anglia, Oxford and Birmingham on such themes as Anglo-Saxon kingship; the kingdom of East Anglia; state formation in northwest Europe; princely burial; barrow cemeteries in England; cemetery forms in the fourth–eighth centuries AD; paganism and Christianity in the seventh century; concepts of wealth in archaeology; and methodological seminars on intensive remote sensing (pre-excavation mapping), 'site geometry' using electronic survey systems and computerized graphics, and chemical enhancement of opaque soils.

*Site evaluation* Following the initial work described above, the first phase of evaluation began with the collection of all the extant records and photographs, which have been transferred to a computerized archive. Woodbridge Museum stimulated local interest by an exhibition to illustrate past, present and projected work. A member of the museum staff turned up a previously unnoticed newspaper cutting from the *Ipswich Journal* of 24 November 1860. 'One of five (*sic*) Roman (*sic*) mounds was opened!' Two bushels of 'iron screw bolts' were recovered, presumably clench-nails from a 'ship-ghost'. They were taken to a local blacksmith, to be made into horseshoes.

In the field, Carver's execution of his design began with clearing the site of all undergrowth – bushes, bracken and other coarse growth. This was done by a team supplied by the local Borstal (a remedial penal institution for young offenders) who have since undertaken to keep the site 'shaved' and therefore much more visible. This enabled a new survey to be made, which identified over 200 former disturbances. These included recent treasure-hunting holes; previous excavations; anti-glider ditches dug in the 1939–45 war; a water-pipe trench; quarrying for golf course bunkers; and disturbances by tanks, who found the mounds a rather exciting course for practice in the war the site was also used as a 2-inch mortar range. New air-photographs were taken, which revealed the presence of at least one unrecorded barrow, now virtually flat but showing up as an area of differential grass and other vegetational growth. Metal detectors were used to clear the area of live shells and other debris of the wartime use of the site. Predictive mapping of underground features was then begun, using electrical resistivity survey, flux-gate gradiometer and magnetic susceptibility, and ground-penetrating radar-pulse survey. All these helped to obtain the maximum amount of data on the site before excavation begun.

A vegetation survey has been mapped, and a detailed contour plan made by electronic distance measurement. Experiments have been made with a viscous compound which it is hoped can consolidate and prevent the erosion of the soft sand, which forms the subsoil of Sutton Hoo and is the principal constituent of the barrows. There has been progress in enhancing the different colorations of the sand, to enable the stains of coffins, bodies, ships, and former wooden features to be seen more clearly. Outside the barrow area, in the nearby ploughed area and wood, trial cuttings have been made which show that archaeological features extend well beyond the known limits of the site.

Environmental studies are looking at pollen, beetles, snails and flora from both buried and present surfaces. There will also be subaquatic exploration of the River Deben opposite Woodbridge, as it is believed that the boats were taken to the site by this route. The work may not only find possible landing places or structures, but also determine the natural topography and environment of the estuary edge in earlier centuries.

It can be seen that these evaluation exercises maximize our understanding of the site without any 'destructive' excavation, and allow the testing of some new and important techniques in dealing with sand sites, in excavation and recording, through chemistry and electronic and computer development.

*Excavation*  When the evaluation exercise had been completed, it was possible to make decisions about how much of the site should be excavated. It was necessary to dig enough of the site to advance materially our understanding, while leaving enough for future generations of archaeologists with better techniques.

The first stage was to explore, in a large excavation, the ploughed field south of the mounds. Here were found extensive prehistoric features and also a dozen very peculiar (flat) graves of the Anglo-Saxon period. The bodies survived as dark stains in the soil, with occasionally some teeth, and other parts of bones existing only rather like soggy blotting paper. It was difficult and tedious to excavate these; each one took one person a week or more to define the ephemeral trace of bodies – 'sand-men' as they came to be called – in three dimensions. Most were in some way or other peculiar – buried face down, decapitated, or in odd positions and diverse orientations.

They were interpreted as 'sinister' burials, executions or sac-rifices, possibly associated with the mound-burials of kings or nobles. One was accompanied by stains of large wooden objects. The whole grave assemblage, as viewed from above, looked like nothing so much as a ploughman in action, seen from the side as a kind of tableau. Was this the grave of some one who had carried out ritual ploughing on the site and was then sacrificed and set out 'in the act'? The sand-men were defined, and then coated, with a latex substance as a 'mould'. From this it was possible to make casts of the 'bodies'. These are now set out on the site, and are a great attraction to visitors.

The next stage was to excavate another big barrow. The one chosen was at the opposite end of the site to that which had been dug in 1939. It was one of the mounds trenched by Basil Brown in 1938, and he had shown that it had been already robbed in antiquity, though he did find interesting remnants in the backfill. There were no hopes here, therefore, of an intact grave and treasure like those of 1939.

Basil Brown's observations were fully confirmed. There had been an enormous trench dug at some unknown time in the past. The robbers had encountered not a boat-burial like the 1939 mound, but a timber-lined burial chamber, like an underground room, with a small boat forming its roof. Such conclusions could be reached by the techniques of modern excavation, even though the earlier diggers had cleared out the chamber very thoroughly. Enough remained, however, to recover the last vestiges of the timber lining of the chamber, and to define the *impressions* made in its base by the array of objects which had been deposited there, with an inhumed body.

Although most of the finds had been removed, many were broken or discarded. Altogether in Basil Brown's trenching and the total excavation of 1987–8, 180 fragments were recovered, from which it will be possible (with the evidence of the impres-sions) to define the outline of the burial layout. The finds are similar in date to those in the 1939 mound, and must originally have been quite as prestigious.

Much was learnt about the method of constructing the mound,

and when it was completely removed, a house of the Beaker period (*c*.2000 BC) was found beneath it – an unexpected bonus.

Two other mounds are currently being excavated; both had been robbed in antiquity, but some evidence survives of the construction methods, and of the rite of cremation.

An important feature of the excavation has been a sustained attempt to involve the public in a programme of explication and education. The BBC have transmitted four programmes on the project, which have attracted over two million viewers. There have also been exhibitions, lectures and site tours organized by the local Sutton Hoo Society.

While the project has made maximum use of available technology in excavation and public education, there is room for further innovation, if resources permitted on a site of this kind. One would be the use of continuous colour video monitoring. This would be invaluable in providing 'action replays' of important stages of the excavation for the archaeologists; but it could also be used to give visitors a close-up view of the actual digging, as if they were looking over the excavator's shoulder. The image could be transmitted by landline across the river to Woodbridge, giving a continuous live coverage of what is happening on the dig. As the work progresses, there may be exciting developments in such techniques as total excavation cover (inflatable buildings with constant light, temperature, humidity and pressure); overhead gantries on which can be hung electrically movable 'cradles' on which excavators can recline, to avoid exerting any pressure by their weight on fragile deposits (perhaps space technology can provide us with a weightless atmosphere so that archaeologists can float around the dig!); freeze-drying on site of crucial deposits so that they can be lifted and transported to a laboratory for dissection; mechanized ways of removing spoil from the site (and bringing it back for site restoration); and developments in three-dimensional colour photography and computer simulation.

Sutton Hoo is an exciting project, and it is hoped that this account will alert readers to follow the final stages of the work through the press and TV.

# Two Case-Studies in British Archaeology

*Earlier work*

Wharram is in a fairly remote area, 40 kilometres northeast of York, on the high chalk of the Yorkshire Wolds, some 30 kilometres from the North Sea coast. The project is concerned not only with the now deserted village of Wharram Percy, but with a wider area of other townships, and with the neighbouring parish of Wharram le Street.

The site is well known in British archaeology and beyond as a deserted medieval village. It is one of many hundreds of such settlements which were flourishing at various times in the Middle Ages, but which were abandoned for various reasons. These have been categorized as, for example, desertions due to the Cistercian monks who 'cleared' rural areas to secure their solitude; to the creation of royal forests for hunting; to the long-term results of fourteenth-century plagues (the Black Death); and to changing economic circumstances, such as the rising price of wool as against corn, which made it possible to run a tract of land with one shepherd, where previously a whole community was engaged in tilling the land.

Not surprisingly, such sites are of great interest to medieval economic historians, and it was one of these, Professor Maurice Beresford, who was the first person to dig at Wharram in 1950. He was attracted to the site because there were very well-defined earthworks, and fairly good medieval documentary sources. He was not an archaeologist, and he dug simply to show that the earthworks did represent medieval peasant buildings. He was interested too in the question of when the village was deserted. He was joined by a Cambridge-trained archaeologist – John Hurst – in 1952, and they continued to collaborate on the site for well over forty years.

Although Wharram began as a medieval village excavation, it has expanded its aims and questions out of all recognition, both in space to include the neighbouring areas (and beyond in some topics), and in time back to the end of the Ice Age and forward to the present. These changes have not come about as a result of

148

a structured developing strategy; they are the result of chance discoveries and reflect also changes in the aims of medieval archaeology. Indeed Wharram can be seen as a microcosm of the development of rural medieval settlement studies during these decades. It has also become well known for the methodological developments that John Hurst has pioneered there, notably that of area excavation, as opposed to the 'grid' or 'box' system developed by Mortimer Wheeler. The essential difference is between a *horizontal* approach – seeing all of one layer at a time – and Wheeler's *vertical* approach, that of studying sections through several layers. The reader is referred to Barker (1977) to understand what this means technically.

For the first twenty years, Wharram was run on a shoe-string budget of a few hundred pounds a year. A band of faithful diggers gathered there each year, paid their own expenses, and gave their help free. This built up a great *esprit de corps* which now extends into the third generation. In 1974, however, Lord Middleton, the owner, generously gave the site to the nation. It became a 'guardianship' site, one of a small number of British sites which are safeguarded from all threats, and for which the new Historic Buildings and Monuments Commission takes responsibility.

The effect of this change was twofold. Firstly, the site now had to be made available for the public to see, as an 'ancient monument'; it had to be maintained, displayed and explained. Secondly, as a result, all excavation, while still research (with few exceptions such as tree-planting threats), was also geared to finding out more about the site, so that some well-preserved structures could be 'laid out' for the public to see, and so that it could be explained to them in an intelligible manner. This is a great challenge. Wharram is not immediately attractive as an ancient monument in the way that castles or abbeys are; there is little to see beyond a ruined church and its churchyard except grass-covered humps and bumps. These mean little to the lay-visitor unless they can be explained.

The work-force, numbering over a hundred at peak times, consists mostly of volunteers and students. Money has also been put into consolidating the church, labelling earthworks by concrete and metal plaques, and the re-creation of the medieval fish-pond by building a new dam across the stream. The outlines of peasant houses that have been dug are indicated by stone slabs, and the plan of long vanished parts of the church is shown by marked-out areas of turf, stone and gravel. Today the site is increasingly attracting tourists, and has a high educational value. There may soon be a site display centre, and perhaps, eventually, even a resident custodian.

### The site

The Wharram site covers a large area, a sheltered valley with a stream running through it, and a windswept terrace or plateau above it. In the valley are the church and churchyard (with its memorial stones), the medieval and later vicarages, two water-mills (known from written sources), the medieval fish-pond and an eighteenth-century farm. Of the farm, three joined cottages survive. These were lived in until *c.*1960, but after that became the excavation headquarters.

On the plateau are numerous peasant houses and two manor houses. All of these are only earthworks, but the outline of walls can be traced, as well as 'hollow ways' which were the routes of communication by foot, animal or cart through the village, and from it to other places. Beyond all these areas of buildings, enclosures and roadways were the open fields cultivated the villagers.

All this is to be seen on the surface, but underneath this are the remains of earlier settlements going back to prehistoric times, which only excavation has revealed. To gain some understanding of how these were discovered, we have to return now to our 'changing problem orientation' and ask how the original question, 'When was the village deserted?' gave way to other, more complex modes of enquiry.

### Changing problems

The first ten years' work were devoted to the very careful excavation of a peasant house. The question of date quickly gave way to research on house structure and on the standard of living of the Wharram peasants, which was surprisingly high to judge by the range and quality of their material possessions, as uncovered by archaeologists.

It was found that the latest house on the site chosen was of the fifteenth century AD, but that below this, in slightly different places and on different orientations, were earlier peasant houses going back to the thirteenth century. High hopes were entertained of carrying the sequence back to Anglo-Saxon times but, very surprisingly, below the earliest peasant house was the filled-in basement or cellar of a well-built stone manor house of the twelfth century (not that represented by other earthworks). The implications were clear: there had been radical changes in village layout during the medieval period, and it could no longer be maintained that the visible earthwork plan was 'as it always had been'.

This was the first major change in Wharram's research direction. The next was the church. Although another peasant house on the plateau was dug (and this did go back to earlier timber structures), the main effort was now on the church.

The settlement as such was abandoned and given over to sheep farming in the fifteenth century, but the church continued to be the place of worship and burial for those of the surrounding settlements that had survived. The last recorded burial was in 1909, and the last service was held in 1949. In the 1950s thieves robbed the roof of its lead and it soon became ruinous. In 1959 half of the tower collapsed, and this was the impetus for the archaeologists to take an interest in the church – another major step away from the peasants and their houses. The rubble was recorded and what remained of the church was made safe from further falls.

The church was totally excavated inside and out, together with associated burials, and the whole structure was drawn stone by stone. The plans of several earlier churches were recovered, and it was shown that the earliest phase, and the earliest burials, were of late Saxon date (though not necessarily contemporary).

The church in its various stages of building, rebuilding, expansion and final contraction was important in its own right as the spiritual nucleus of the settlement for many centuries. But it was

151

also a microcosm of the changing fortunes of both the village and its lords. It also provided the first data, in the form of skeletons, on the villagers and lords themselves, and on their priests. These data were able to give information on public health and nutrition, age expectancy, infant mortality and disease. Over 600 graves have now been dug, out of a total of 5000–8000 people who are estimated to have been buried at Wharram. Of these, only a maximum of thirty-eight are now marked by memorial stones (Rahtz and Watts, 1983).

Horizons were expanded further when, below the lowest church levels, pottery was found of the Iron Age and Roman periods, showing that Wharram did not originate as a medieval village. Further work in the valley during the 1970s included a large excavation of the medieval fish-pond dam and, below this, the remains of the millponds of Saxon date, though all remains of the actual mills had been destroyed, swept away by flooding or removed by later medieval structures such as the fishponds. These excavations widened the scope of enquiry into the technology of milling and fish-farming. Further excavations carried the Wharram story forward in time into the post-medieval centuries with the study of the eighteenth-century vicarage and farm. Details of these, recovered by archaeology, correspond with and corroborate (but vastly enlarge on) the details given in contemporary written sources.

These large-scale excavations had been very informative about particular areas and structures, but there were still large parts of the site about which nothing was known. The change to guardianship status gave greater opportunities to explore more widely, and in the 1970s a series of trial trenches was dug in many parts of the village. The results were startling. Not only did they reveal widespread evidence of Anglo–Saxon, Roman and Iron Age occupation, but they showed that the very plan of the earthworks, which had been assumed to be a medieval creation, had its origins in the Roman and prehistoric periods. Roman ditches and banks were found to underlie medieval ones, and a major linear boundary marking the ends of peasant properties was shown to be a prehistoric field bank. It was now clear that Wharram had been intensively occupied for at least a thousand years before the medieval village and its earthworks which had sparked off the original research. The great attraction for settlers was probably the excellent water supply.

The next stage was the realization that, however interesting all this might be for the 'site' of Wharram Percy (whose limits were now by no means so certain as they had been), we needed to see if the site was typical of the area, and to set it into a wider context. This was done in two ways: intensive aerial photography which showed in soil crop-marks the outlines of former fields, settlements and buildings; and systematic walking over all the ploughed fields within 5 kilometres of Wharram Percy. Pottery and other finds of all periods were picked up and their positions mapped. This helped to date the air-photograph markings, and to plot the position and extent of occupation in different places in the Iron Age, Roman, Saxon and medieval periods.

By these two methods of non-excavational field-work among other sites, two Roman villas were discovered, both within 2 kilometres of Wharram Percy itself. Fragments of mosaic, painted plaster, tiles from heating systems, and other finds indicated the high status of these sites. It was realized that settlement in the area in the Roman period may have been more intensive than at any time before or since.

A further technique was now employed to find out more about the villas. A survey of both sites was done using a magnetometer. This is a device which measures the magnetic response of buried finds and features. It can pick up hearths, ditches, pits, walls, roads and other features by recording their different magnetic response to that of the natural chalk. It was possible in both cases to recover the extent and entire plan of both sites in outline, though not to date the individual components (figure 6 indicates the result from one of the villas).

A further stage was to excavate a series of small holes on both villas. In only four days and with a dozen workers, the evidence of field-walking, aerial photography and magnetometer survey was much enhanced. Elements of the buildings were found which showed the range of materials used and the dating range. Ditches were sectioned to find their depth and date; and again prehistoric occupation was proved, extending back, in the case of

*Figure 6* Wharram-le-Street, North Yorkshire: magnetometer survey of Roman villa site, 1978

the villa illustrated, to Mesolithic flints dating to thousands of years before the Roman period (Rahtz et al., 1986).

*Training and theory*

The Wharram project has provided useful expertise for students. Here, in the summer season, they learn how to excavate and draw, fill out recording forms and process the thousands of finds of all kinds, from pottery to animal bones. But because it is part of an academic course, and not just a field school in practical archaeology, an attempt has been made to express the whole Wharram project in a theoretical framework, shown here as figure 7.

Concepts such as those expressed in the diagram help students to gain a perspective of the whole project and its importance, even when what they are doing day by day is only a tiny fragment of the whole. Figure 7 represents a *systemic* approach to the massive Wharram data, rather than a *chronological* one. Here we're not dealing successively with Iron Age people, Romans, Saxons and medieval peasants and lords, but with the systems that operate within society, each of them having complex links and interaction with others.

Such systems and their interaction may be seen in modern society. In York, the city runs through the efficient management of many interlinking systems: the legal system with its police and courts; the ecclesiastical systems of its cathedral and churches; the commercial systems of banking and commerce; the academic systems of its university and schools; its social systems of heat, light, sewage, hospitals and welfare; the trading systems dealing with long-distance luxury imports (such as Japanese TV sets) and its mundane food and drink, distributed on a more local basis and involved in a complex symbiosis with the rural hinterland.

Add to these the systems of transport, industry and (in York especially) tourism and archaeology, and we begin to build a theoretical framework to explain how York works. It would be relatively straightforward to depict present-day York systems, and one could from written sources build up a similar framework (changing all the time) back through the nineteenth and eight-

*Figure 7* Wharram data and interpretation

eenth centuries to Tudor times. As we go further back through time, written sources become more sparse, and for medieval, Viking and Roman York, the archaeologists hope to build a picture of York's earlier systems based almost wholly on archaeological evidence. It would in York be far more complex than that for Wharram, but similar in the type of theoretical framework within which the data are considered.

*Current work*

The year 1990 saw the completion of forty years of work on the site. The occasion was marked by festivities, including the presentation of a book of essays to John Hurst and Maurice Beresford in celebration of their long partnership; and the publication of a book by them summing up the results of this long campaign (Beresford and Hurst, 1990).

Future work will be concentrated on other sites in the area, to provide a context for the intensive work on the site itself; this will be under the direction of a new body, the Wharram Research Committee. Meanwhile Wharram will remain as a monument, a unique opportunity for the general public to see and study all aspects of a prehistoric, Roman, Saxon and medieval settlement in its chronological and landscape setting. Most of what will be visible will be of medieval date. The experience of visiting Wharram will be a valuable counterbalance to the partial impression people get of medieval daily life by visiting castles, religious houses and other major buildings which were used only by the few.

# 9

# Archaeology and the Public

Archaeology has a series of different publics at varying levels of appreciation. All of them put together are a very small minority of the population. The dialogue between archaeologists and their publics is complex in motive, media and method. The vast majority of the public are not only not interested in archaeology as a method of understanding the past, they are not interested in the past. A farmer on Sanday (one of the north isles of Orkney, an area where one might expect an interest in tradition and 'old days') confessed to me (or rather asserted) that he was more interested in the future: in 'computers, space, and the supernatural'. This did not stop him from being very helpful to the archaeologists digging on his land.

The relatively small proportion of people who are interested in the past vary in their response to archaeology according to two principal factors – the skill with which archaeologists communicate or expound their subject, and the very diverse levels of public perception about what lies behind present experience. We have already seen the aboriginal concept of only two 'times', the moving present and the ancestral past, and it is doubtful whether the majority of people, even in an educated country like Britain, have more than this dual conception of time. 200 years ago, 20,000, 200,000, 2 million, all are much the same in public perception, though critically different for the archaeologist (Lowenthal, 1985). Film audiences are not disturbed by watching

158

Raquel Welch and other early hominids co-inhabiting a landscape with dinosaurs and pterodactyls, in *One Million Years BC*; or Romans fighting Vikings in *The Viking Queen*.

At the academic level there are only a few hundred people likely to read or skim most of the papers or monographs written on archaeology. An important book with a wide scholarly appeal such as *Models in Archaeology* (Clarke, 1972), with a wider market in the USA and elsewhere, might sell a few thousand copies. At a more popular level, the book you are reading will be doing well if it reaches a world readership of 10,000, a very small proportion of the world's population, and minute compared to the books of the 'alternative archaeology' (chapter 7).

Interest in archaeology is not, however, confined to those who read books. The public which archaeology tries to serve and communicate with is potentially the much wider one whose members listen to radio, watch television, travel and look at 'ancient monuments', visit museums and look at excavations. The numbers in Britain are possibly a million or two who can be reached in some way. Beyond this there is the great majority, who do none of these things. Most are apathetic to archaeology, or downright hostile when it is seen in their view to be 'wasting public money' or delaying 'progress'. When I was digging the Saxon and medieval palaces of Cheddar, I was held by some of the village community to be delaying the new school (the building of this was the reason for the dig). One of the village councillors said, 'They say they've found King Alfred's palace. Now he was a great believer in education, if he was here he'd say get on with the school' – which was probably true! At the very best, we may cite the recent instance of the estimated British audience of 2.5 million who watched the breakfast-time saga of the lifting of the Tudor warship *Mary Rose* from the seabed; or the programmes on Sutton Hoo.

Half a million, then, is probably our maximum potential public at the most popular level; so far, we as archaeologists have been singularly unsuccessful in getting over to them the real interest of archaeology which I hope I have sketched in this book. The reasons for this are discussed later in this chapter. There are many different levels at which we may hope to make any impact. These levels depend on how our public *perceives* archaeology. Generally the perception is low-key: archaeology is 'about digging up old things, especially treasure'; in many people's minds it's something that happens in other countries, especially in Greece or Egypt. Above all it is *mysterious*. At a higher key, *local* archaeology has a considerable appeal, and so do *finds* of all kinds, especially human skeletons.

The public are often puzzled by things they see on digs or hear in lectures. One of the most common questions from visitors is, 'How did all this get buried?' The simple answer here is earthworms, who cast up dirt on any exposed surface at an astonishing rate – one can observe how quickly a path gets buried if not regularly cleared. There is also some material derived from leaves, weeds and frost, which help the earthworm to bury our past.

Although we seem to dig up a lot of people's past rubbish, most of it does *not* get buried, but dispersed and reused or destroyed. What we find is a minute fraction of what was used in the past. Future generations will be more lucky – we put our rubbish in huge dumps, from which the future archaeologists will have a vast harvest of bottles, tins, bedsteads, washing machines and television sets; they will also have a massive documentary record of what these things mean in our society, if our paper, film and magnetic tape survive. If they don't, the rubbish dumps will be the only source from which our life can be reconstructed, as is the case now for our own prehistory.

Why should we try to reach the public? Why should we not be content to be a minority group, appealing to a small elite, who will appreciate to the full our methods and our subtle approaches to the past?

We do need an informed public; we cannot afford to be isolated. Archaeology needs the understanding and collaboration of the farmer, the gravel-extractor and the bushman. An informed and interested public will not destroy its own past (our raw data). Legislation to protect monuments or provide resources for archaeology cannot be effective without public support. Local authorities, planning committees and builders must see archaeology as a resource, as strengthening community identity with its region and its heritage. Modern social mobility threatens our roots; archaeology can help us to renew a sense of context without risking the disasters of parochialism or nationalism.

Archaeology is potentially a source of tourist income. Public interest must extend to MPs. Why do birds, poetry, painting and the theatre rank higher in public awareness and priority for government grants? Why is Japan the biggest archaeological spender per head of the population?

We need public support in all places and at all levels. Readers of this book who have followed me so far will, I hope, have no doubts about the intrinsic interest of archaeology, and its importance in today's world, but we may recapitulate some of the reason why we should try to get a bigger public, at the risk of some repetition.

EDUCATION OR ENTERTAINMENT?

The wider the public we wish to involve, the more popular our approach must be. It is difficult, however, to lower our sights without vulgarizing, trivializing or being downright misleading. At worst, in efforts to entertain, some writers and TV presenters have descended to sensationalism or personalization, pandering to the big demand for features on treasure, mummies, skeletons or mystery. The real excitement of archaeology is a formidable concept to put over in any medium.

Formal education is one way of preparing the ground. From the primary school onwards, the tangible and practical aspects of archaeology, in the classroom or outside in town or country, provide excellent opportunities for the teacher, broadening and deepening the base of history. Many teachers are as uninformed about archaeology as the majority of the public, and since the public's image of archaeology is as a harmless hobby, with odd people digging up things, neither education ministers, committees, school heads or teachers are likely to treat archaeology as an important and eminently suitable subject for the curriculum. A hopeful development is, however, the acceptance of archaeology as a *separate subject* (not part of history) in the National Curriculum. The Council for British Archaeology, through their education officer, have designed syllabi and examinations for this purpose, which it is hoped will gradually create an informed public.

In secondary education the position in Britain is rather better. It is possible to take GCSE and A-level archaeology, and the standards are high; but there are not enough teachers able to take the subject on, or school heads eager to introduce the subject and find someone to teach it. It was hoped at one time that archaeology might fill the gap in humanist studies left by the decline in classical studies, or that it might take a slice of the history cake; but neither of these things has happened, though valiant attempts are being made. In history, even medieval topics are rarely taught after the first year; Tudors and Stuarts and the nineteenth century still reign supreme – a very small and recent part of Britain's past.

We are left with tertiary education, with twenty or thirty universities in Britain offering various degrees, in archaeology by itself or in conjunction with other appropriate subjects, especially history and, to a lesser extent, geology or geography. Some universities, notably Bradford, have an important scientific bias, and offer BSc rather than BA degrees. For the very best students, there are ample opportunities for postgraduate research. Few students know very much about archaeology when they come from school; perhaps 5 per cent have taken archaeology GCSE or A-level. Thirty per cent or more have, however, 'been on a dig', and this is usually crucial in having persuaded them to read archaeology.

The range of courses available is very wide, from scientific archaeology to historically based studies, from the earliest hominids and stone tools to post-medieval archaeology and ethno-archaeology, and from British-based courses to ones that cover the archaeology of more distant areas, especially northwest Europe and the Mediterranean, but including Egypt, the Far East, Polynesia, Australia and the Americas. Readers of this book who are thinking of studying archaeology should make themselves well informed about what is on offer.

An informed public is essential if archaeology is to survive as a subject, and equally importantly if its subject-matter, its sites above and below ground, are to survive the destructive agencies of nature and modern industrial society. Debates about the provision of resources for archaeology at local authority or central government level are frighteningly ill informed.

It is not surprising, therefore, that public knowledge of archaeology is so slight, compared with that in some other countries, notably Scandinavia, Holland and Switzerland. The subject can only be promoted in the future by the few hundred graduates turned out by British universities each year. They can, and do, do a great deal to make people around them better informed, by talking and teaching. Those that get into jobs in archaeology can do a great deal more, in campaigning for more resources, awakening local authorities to the value of their archaeological heritage, persuading farmers and metal-detectorists not to destroy the past wantonly for the sake of profit, and monitoring or hopefully recording the ravages of nature.

SANDAY

An excellent example of what can be done at the local level is provided by the north Orkney isle of Sanday. It has a population of just over 500. Like most of Orkney it is extremely rich in archaeological sites, ranging from Neolithic chambered tombs through Bronze Age, Pictish and Norse settlement sites to its medieval and modern farms. Many of the farms are on or near the sites of their predecessors. Unlike some of the better-known Orkney islands, which are extensively visited by tourists, and with famous sites (such as the Neolithic village of Skara Brae, the Neolithic tomb of Maes Howe, and stone circles), Sanday was hardly known to tourists, and its archaeology was until recently neglected. It was left to the Orkney field archaeologist, Raymond Lamb, to survey the island, talk to its farmers and make them aware of their island history. What makes Sanday unique, and gives the island its name, are the extensive dunes and areas of blown sand which have buried well-preserved ancient sites. In places this has happened several times, so that there are up to 2–3

163

metres of archaeological deposits extending through four thousand years. There are also many large mounds of soil and midden deposits, rather like the settlement mounds ('tells') of the Middle East, which have either been built up deliberately or have accumulated through time. On and in these are the well-preserved stone structures of Norse and later farms.

All this rich archaeology is being steadily destroyed, not by the farmers of Sanday, but by the sea. Huge storms sweeping in from the Atlantic whip up great waves, which not only sometimes flood the coastal farms, but tear into the low cliffs and into their deep archaeological deposits. In one winter, up to 10 metres of land has been lost in places, representing thousands of tons of archaeological levels. To Lamb this was a situation that demanded action. With the goodwill secured by his public relations exercise with the Sanday people, he arranged for a large-scale dig to be done by John Hunter of the University of Bradford. Hunter opened quite large areas behind the sea-eroded cliff, and demonstrated the great potential of the site in Pictish and Norse times, with well-preserved stone buildings and a wealth of artefacts.

The islanders were impressed and convinced about their island's past. When the dig was finished, Hunter produced an illustrated report in the form of a four-page newspaper. A copy of this was delivered to every home on the island. A conference of Scottish archaeologists was held on Sanday for five days. The warmth of the islanders' hospitality and the extent of their interest in archaeology was a remarkable experience. Many of the islanders came round with us on our excursions and thirty or forty of them came to the lectures in their village hall on all aspects of their past, from the Neolithic tombs and settlements to the Jacobite rebellion in Orkney, and modern farming practice. Of especial interest to them was the archaeological evidence for the production of kelp, which brought great wealth to Orkney, and Sanday in particular, in the later eighteenth and early nineteenth centuries. Seaweed was burnt to produce an ashy residue used in glass-making, and later in the manufacture of iodine.

Sanday is an example of what can be done at a *local* level, but is of little help in reaching our wider potential audience or public.

## MEDIA, MUSEUMS AND MONUMENTS

### *Media*

Formal education and public relations exercises like Sanday can lay foundations for a public interest in archaeology, but they have limited scope. The more indirect role of public presentation is potentially vastly greater, especially through the media, which can reach virtually the whole world population in one way or another. But the media are under the control neither of archaeologists nor even of academics, who may in any case be quite unqualified to put archaeology across.

In Britain, newspapers report archaeology in a very small way, principally at the local level – the local find or dig, emphasizing the sensational or the personal. Even when an archaeologist gives the reporter a careful tour of the dig, or gives him or her a written account, the result after editing is seldom satisfactory, or even accurate. Even *The Guardian* and the *Telegraph*, in reporting the remarkable find in York of an eighth-century Anglo-Saxon helmet, managed to turn it into a *Viking* helmet in their columns. Sunday colour supplements have been of great value in carrying illustrated reports of big excavations such as York or London and crises in the funding of British archaeology, or in the destruction of the archaeological heritage. We have some good allies here.

Radio has put out several series on archaeology. The producer of the BBC *Origins* programme claims to have a big audience. In a lecture in York, he played extracts from programmes to persuade the audience that the spoken word can convey visual images to the listener as successfully as can television or film.

There has yet to be a full-scale commercial film which deals successfully with archaeology. Archaeologists figure as very odd characters in films like *Raiders of the Lost Ark*, which *did* reach a world audience, and *does* depict archaeology being done, even if with the worst of motives and with appallingly crude methods. Most 'archeaological' films are highly imaginative reconstructions of the past (or the future), especially of Vikings, Egyptians or Romans, often, as we have seen, with scant regard for time-sense.

165

Television is potentially the archaeologist's most effective shop-window. Series such as Kenneth Clark's *Civilisation*, Bronowski's *The Ascent of Man* and Leakey's *The Making of Mankind* (Leakey, 1981) have reached world audiences of many millions. David Attenborough, in his *Life on Earth*, *The Living Planet* and *Trials of Life*, has been enormously successful in depicting both the history of people's environment and animal life, but he has yet to turn his hand to the history of humankind; if he did so, we could be assured of a vast public eager to know more. The BBC's *Chronicle* series were notable in former years, but have recently become less effective, with certain notable exceptions, such as Barry Cunliffe's programme on Bath. None of the current series, however, gets anywhere near the enormous success of *Animal, Vegetable and Mineral*, in which Mortimer Wheeler became a household name, and which people still remember many years later. Wheeler did more than any other single person to popularize archaeology, without ever descending to sensationalism or historical inaccuracy.

The BBC did make one serious attempt to explain the approaches and methods of archaeology in their sustained reporting of the excavation at Silbury Hill, the great ceremonial mound in Wiltshire. This was regarded by their producers as a successful educational venture, although 'nothing was found' in any way that might be thought to appeal to a wide public. Peter Fowler may have been underestimating the public when he suggested that the only way to have put Silbury over would have been for the BBC to 'plant' in the middle of the mound a 'royal mummy, swathed in gold lamé, and containing a pregnant child-bride richly attired, murdered and headless'.

One Channel 4 series, too, attempted to get over serious points. This was *The Blood of the British*. The front person here was Dr Catherine Hills of the University of Cambridge, who is an academic of very high standing, and also happens to be extremely good to look at. The critics named her at once 'the thinking man's pin-up'. Her theme in the programmes was that there is an underlying continuity of 'British' population throughout the millennia; and that the changes from, say, Bronze Age to Iron Age were ones of culture and technology rather than new people; that underneath a veneer of Roman, Anglo-Saxon, Viking or Normal political and military control, the same old British formed the bulk of the population – ploughing, working and reproducing themselves.

## Museums

Museums have traditionally been the institutions where the public went if they wanted to know about the past. For over a century they have fulfilled this role with varying success. Most are still object-orientated, giving the impression that the past is represented by finds rather than being about the understanding of settlement or the environment. The finds were and are often in glass cases, untouchable and remote, with little explanation. Especial emphasis is given to rich finds of gold and silver, and other exotic materials. To the academic archaeologist, these displays are of great interest, and we visit museums all over the world to see this material culture. The more old-fashioned, crowded and unselective the display the more we like it (within limits); the more there is to study, photograph, and note. But for the public, this is a quite ineffective mode of stimulation or enlightenment. If you doubt this, sit in a gallery in one of the more archaic museums and watch the public drift by as though they were only sheltering from the rain (they probably are). Lord Montagu, Chairman of the English Tourist Board, was well aware of this when he attacked Britain's top museums. He dismissed their curators as 'crusty and pompous'; 'the more honours they have, the duller they are.'

Things are, however, looking up. More and more museums have lots of pictures, explanations, brilliant display and lighting, audiovisual displays, models of excavations, and reconstructions in pictures or three dimensions of early buildings or settlements. Notable here are the great ship museums, the National Maritime Museum at Greenwich, the Oslo Ship Museum, that at Roskilde in Denmark, and the museum built around the seventeenth-century warship *Wasa* at Stockholm. The public also feel especially drawn to museums of more recent times, with which they

167

can identify, such as the ever-popular Castle Museum in York, which includes a complete nineteenth-century street with its shops, and a vast collection of 'bygones'. Also in York is the great National Railway Museum, with huge shining locomotives and evocative displays of the Age of Steam.

However good these displays are, they are none the less static, with at best a few science museum working models, or coin-in-the-slot 'scenes', such as the grisly public execution in York Castle Museum. The new museum concept is very different, and will be vastly more effective in public education, as I have mentioned in relation to Sturbridge Old Village (pages 20–1) and the Jorvik Viking Centre. The latter was created by a new breed of museum men, 'leisure engineers' or, as they call themselves, 'imagineers'. At its opening we were given some of the first rides in the time-cars, and then treated to a magnificent feast provided and flown in by Iceland Air: superb Icelandic fish, roast lamb, curd and blueberries. Our host was another successful front person, Magnus Magnusson, himself an Icelander.

The Jorvik Viking Centre was only the beginning. A similar project was mounted at Canterbury, about Chaucer's Pilgrims and the Canterbury Tales; another at Oxford on the history of the university. One of the most successful concerned more recent times – the Industrial Revolution; at Ironbridge Gorge one is introduced to the whole of working-class life in the iron and steel industry. There is a complete village with people in costume playing their parts, as at Sturbridge. The visitor to the school sits in a hard desk and is belaboured by a shouting schoolmaster – this is 'interactive' entertainment. At Plymouth we have the 'Armada Experience'; at Liverpool what it was like to emigrate to the New World in the nineteenth century. At Tamworth, there will be King Offa's Hall with Saxons feasting, and a full-scale working watermill based on my excavation there (page 98).

The largest such project of all is now available at Dover (page 20). Concerned at the possible decline of the town when the Channel Tunnel is operational, Dover District Council decided to attract tourists to Dover by means of a heritage centre, the White Cliffs Experience, illustrating the whole history of Dover from its prehistoric and Roman origins to its premier importance as terminus of the shortest Channel crossing. A unique feature of this £14-million enterprise is a long-running archaeological dig of the Roman fort of the Channel Fleet (the *Classis Britannica*) and the later fort which defended the south coast against Germanic pirates. The visitors to the centre will be able to see archaeologists at work over many years, from digging to publication, and have it all explained to them.

All this proliferating activity will do much to educate the public; this has been dubbed *The Heritage Industry* by Robert Hewison (1987), who sees in all this a form of escapism from the reality of the present – a sort of nostalgia for past golden ages which never in fact existed.

## Monuments

What of the *real* monuments of our past? Compared to the imaginative creations described above, they are archaic in their appeal to the public. To quote Peter Addyman, the Director of the York Archaeological Trust:

> Almost all of the 399 national monuments are crying out for this kind of treatment, but the imagination has not been there. We have convinced ourselves that we have a duty to put the heritage across in an interesting and exciting away. It belongs to all of us, and it is too important to be left to the scholars, the museums, and the experts with unreadable guide books.

English Heritage aims to make our heritage understood by all, and to make it *pay* – even though the aims are rather contrasting in their ethics.

However successful we are or may be in promoting understanding of archaeology or of the past, we are not reaching or going to reach the great majority, those who *don't* go to the Jorvik Viking Centre, who *pass* the doors of museums, who *switch off* the radio or TV when there is anything even remotely cultural. We write for the *Observer*, *The Guardian*, the *Telegraph*,

*The Times*; but not for the *Sun*, *Star*, or *Mirror*. Here we may justly be accused of being elitist. This may be one reason for the hostility shown to archaeology not only by the irrationalists, but by the metal-detectorists.

It may well be that archaeology is on the verge of a big boom, as there is growing leisure and a search for roots and a 'natural' past in an increasingly contaminated and industrialized world. The problems of saturation visiting of monuments, their wearing away by millions of feet, however distasteful this may be to the high-minded archaeologist, are probably less worrying than the gradual disappearance of any interest in the past or its heritage, and the exclusive concentration on today's and tomorrow's material world.


## ARCHAEOLOGY AND YOU

Readers of this book are a small minority. They already have enough interest in archaeology to buy or borrow it. I hope that the book has increased this initial interest, and promoted an incentive to enquire further; or even to become personally involved.

A wider understanding can be achieved by watching all television programmes on archaeology and listening to those on radio. The next step would be to subscribe to archaeological periodicals (see pages 174–5), notably (in Britain) *Current Archaeology* and *British Archaeological News*. For a wider world coverage, *Antiquity* is strongly recommended.

The place to find out more about opportunities in archaeology, and especially those in your own area, is the local museum or library. They will often be able to provide details of continuing education courses in archaeology, and of lectures, excursions, conferences and local societies; joining one of the last of these will put you in touch with the archaeological activities in the area, and lead to participation in field-work, excavation or museum work.

There are many opportunities in archaeology for those with special skills, such as survey, photography or drawing. Archaeological excavations welcome volunteers who can work in all weathers and at short notice.

You may, however, wish to go further and be a profesional archaeologist, in the sense of getting paid to do archaeology. It used to be possible to get into archaeology without any training or qualifications (as I did). In Britain this has become increasingly difficult, but there may well be openings in other countries where there is a shortage of archaeologists. To get any further in Britain, you have to have a lot of experience, publications and reputation, which are difficult to acquire, or you must embark on training. We have seen in chapter 4 how to do this, and in chapter 5 what it is like to be a student. Not all students are fresh from school. Some are 'mature' students, of all ages from 21 to 50+. Graduation takes three years, and there are postgraduate courses, such as museum studies at Leicester. If you are talented and motivated enough you may work your way into an archaeological career, as a digger or field-worker, a museum curator, a local authority archaeologist, or an academic.

171

# Conclusion

Many readers of this book, even if they have found it stimulating and enjoyable, will not have found in it the answers to all the questions in their minds when they bought or borrowed it. Many important aspects of archaeology are hardly mentioned, notably the practical aspects – tools, techniques, stratigraphy, survey and other things inseparable from modern archaeology. There is little on finds, or on the many scientific and specialist skills which are increasingly being brought to bear on our evidence. There are many new kinds of archaeology which the reader of this book may remain unaware of, such as industrial and marine (underwater) archaeology. I can only repeat that this is not meant to be a textbook, but a personal view of the relevance of archaeology to the world of today. Readers who want to find out how to 'do' archaeology are referred to other books listed below.

The only missing chapter which I would like to have written is 'archaeology in the future', if indeed it has one. I have written about today's rubbish, but not how future archaeologists will deal with it. Speculation here really belongs to the world of science fiction, and certain developments are hinted at in chapter 7. I shall not be here to see the exciting developments that the twenty-first century will bring to our discipline, on this Earth or beyond. But I hope that there are enough young readers to see these new things happen, and to be able to look back at this book and say 'this is what it was like in the 1990s.'

# Further Reading

Leslie Alcock *Arthur's Britain* (Penguin, Harmondsworth, 1974): this will help you to understand the Dark Age sections in this book.

David Baker *Living with the Past* (David Baker, Bedford, 1984): a lively book on the problems of caring for the historic environment in modern planning.

Philip Barker *Techniques of Archaeological Excavation* (Batsford, London, 1977): a classic book on the complexity and subtlety of modern excavation.

John Coles *Experimental Archaeology* (Academic Press, London, 1979): few archaeologists try, as Coles does, to find out how things worked in the past; modern replicas are made of weapons, buildings are erected and burnt down, to gain more understanding of the evidence that archaeologists find.

James Deetz *Invitation to Archaeology* (Natural History Press, New York, 1967): this book's namesake, and still a very good introduction to modern theoretical archaeology.

Angela Evans *The Sutton Hoo Ship-Burial: A Handbook* (British Museum, London, 1986). A readable account of the 1939 finds and later work to supplement the discussion in chapter 8.

Peter Fowler *Approaches to Archaeology* (Black, London, 1977): A lively and entertaining book and one of the first to explore some of the topics developed in this volume.

Kevin Greene *Archaeology: An Introduction* (Batsford, London, 1983): very readable.

# Further Reading

Barri Jones *Past Imperfect – The Story of Rescue Archaeology* (Heinemann, London, 1984): the problems faced by archaeologists in the 1960s and 1970s as they saw their evidence being destroyed faster than it could be recorded.

Richard Leakey *The Making of Mankind* (Michael Joseph, London, 1981): the book of the BBC series; how and why humankind began, and whether we will prove to be a short-lived species.

Bryony Orme *Anthropology for Archaeologists* (Duckworth, London, 1981): an introduction to the relationship between these two subjects.

Philip Rahtz (ed.) *Rescue Archaeology* (Penguin, Harmondsworth, 1974): how our achaeological heritage was being destroyed twenty years ago; it is still being eroded by the same agencies of humankind and nature.

Colin Renfrew *Before Civilisation* (Penguin, Harmondsworth, 1973): the *big* perspective, showing the dramatic impact of modern radiocarbon dating.

Andrew Sherratt (ed.) *The Cambridge Encyclopaedia of Archaeology* (Cambridge University Press, Cambridge, 1980): an even *bigger* perspective on humankind in space and time, covering the world for five million years.

Mortimer Wheeler *Archaeology from the Earth* (Clarendon Press, Oxford, 1954): although forty years old, this book shows Wheeler's tremendous flair and capacity to communicate.

*Current Archaeology*: obtainable by subscription (six issues a year, £12, post free) from 9 Nassington Road, London NW3 2TX. This is the best magazine for keeping in touch with the latest discoveries; very lively and well produced, it gives details of local societies, and of how to become members of the Council for Independent Archaeology, which organizes regular conferences for independent archaeologists, and offers a service of specialist help to those who do not have the benefit of the resources of a professional organization.

*British Archaeological News*: obtainable by subscription (six issues a year, £10, post free) from the Council for British Archaeology, 112 Kennington Road, London SE11 6RE. Both *Current Archaeology* and *British Archaeological News* provide a commentary on what is going on in the politics of British archaeology, and details of awards, prizes and – most usefully – details of excavations or summer schools which you can join, even as a beginner, and possibly get part of the costs of food or travel reimbursed.

*Antiquity*: obtainable by subscription (four issues a year, £25, post free) from Oxford Journals, Pinkhill House, Southfield Road, Eynsham OX8 1JJ. This is a lively and well-produced survey of archaeology in all parts of the world.

# Bibliography

Adams, D. 1979: *The Hitch-Hiker's Guide to the Galaxy*. Pan: London.

Alcock, L. 1974: *Arthur's Britain*. Penguin: Harmondsworth.

Ashe, G. 1979: *The Glastonbury Tor Maze*. Gothic Fringe: Glastonbury.

Asimov, I. 1974: *Foundation*. Panther: St Albans.

Auel, J. 1980: *The Clan of the Cave Bear*. Book Club Associates: London.

Auel, J. 1982: *The Valley of the Horses*. Book Club Associates: London.

Auel, J. 1986: *The Mammoth Hunters*. Book Club Associates: London.

Auel, J. 1990: *The Plains of Passage*. Hodder and Stoughton: London.

Bailey, R., Cambridge, E. and Briggs, H.D. 1988: *Dowsing in Church Archaeology*. Intercept: Wimborne.

Barker, P.A. 1977: *Techniques of Archaeological Excavation*. Batsford: London.

Beresford, M. and Hurst, J. 1990: *Wharram Percy*. English Heritage/Batsford: London.

Bonnichsen, R. 1973: Millie's Camp: An Experiment in Archaeology. *World Archaeology*, 4.3, 277–91.

Boulle, P. 1966: *Monkey Planet*. Penguin: London.

Bruce-Mitford, R. 1975–83: *The Sutton Hoo Ship Burial*. Three volumes. British Museum: London.

Burrow, I. 1983: The Glastonbury Zodiac. *Popular Archaeology*, 4 (8), 28–31.

Butzer, K. 1982: *Archaeology as Human Ecology*. Cambridge University Press: Cambridge.

Chippindale, C. (ed.) 1989: *Who Owns Stonehenge?* Batsford: London.

Clark, G. 1965: *Archaeology and Society*. Methuen: London.

Clarke, D.L. (ed.) 1972: *Models in Archaeology*. Methuen: London.

Daniel, G.E. 1975: *150 Years of Archaeology*. Duckworth: London.

# Bibliography

Davies, N. 1979: *Voyagers to the New World: Fact or Fantasy?* Publisher and place of publication not known.

Deetz, J. 1967: *Invitation to Archaeology*. Natural History Press: New York.

Evans, A. 1986: *The Sutton Hoo Ship-Burial: A Handbook*: British Museum: London.

Fagan, B.M. 1978: Chairman Mao's Archaeology. In Fagan, *Quest for the Past*, Addison-Wesley: London, 261–81.

Golding, W. 1955: *The Inheritors*. Faber and Faber: London.

Hawkes, J. 1982: *Mortimer Wheeler, Adventurer in Archaeology*. Weidenfeld and Nicolson: London.

Hewison, R. 1987: *The Heritage Industry: Britain in a Climate of Decline*. Methuen: London.

Hodder, I. 1982: *The Present Past*. Batsford: London.

Hubert, J. 1988: A Proper Place for the Dead. In R. Layton (ed.), *Conflict in the Archaeology of Living Traditions*, Unwin Hyman: London, 131–65.

*Journal of Galactic Archaeology* (first issue awaiting data).

Kennedy, G. 1983: *Invitation to Statistics*. Martin Robertson: Oxford.

Kilworth, G. 1975: Let's Go to Gologotha. In *The Gollancz/Sunday Times Best SF Stories*, Gollancz/Sunday Times: London.

Leakey, R.E. 1981: *The Making of Mankind*. Michael Joseph: London.

Lodge, D. 1965: *The British Museum is Falling Down*. Penguin: Harmondsworth.

Lowenthal, D. 1985: *The Past is a Foreign Country*. Cambridge University Press: Cambridge.

Macaulay, D. 1979: *The Motel of the Mysteries*. Hutchinson: London.

Maltwood, K.A. 1935: *A Guide to Glastonbury's Temple of the Stars*. Privately published: London.

Maltwood, K.A. 1937: *Air View Supplement to Maltwood 1935*. Privately published: London.

Mongait, A.L. 1961: *Archaeology in the USSR*. Penguin: Harmondsworth.

Phahtz, R. 1985: The Wharram Percy Memorial Stones: An Anthropological View from Mars. In D. Hooke (ed.), *Medieval Villages*, monograph no. 5, Oxford University Committee for Archaeology: Oxford, 215–25.

Radford, C.A.R. and Swanton, M.J. 1975: Tintagel. In Radford and Swanton, *Arthurian Sites in the West*, University of Exeter: Exeter, 16–24.

Rahtz, P. 1964: Excavations at Chalice Well, Glastonbury. *Proceedings of the Somerset Archaeological and Natural History Society*, 108, 145–63.

Rahtz, P.A. 1971: Excavations on Glastonbury Tor 1964–66. *Archaeological Journal*, 127, 1–81.

Rahtz, P.A. (ed.) 1974: *Rescue Archaeology*. Penguin: Harmondsworth.

Rahtz, P.A. 1979a: *The Saxon and Medieval Palaces at Cheddar*. British Archaeological Reports 65. British Archaeological Reports: Oxford.

Rahtz, P.A. 1979b: Sutton Hoo Opinions – Forty Years On. In P. Rahtz, T. Dickinson and L. Watts (eds.), *Anglo-Saxon Cemeteries 1979*, British Archaeological Reports 82, British Archaeological Reports: Oxford, 313–370.

Rahtz, P.A. 1981: Medieval Milling. In D.W. Crossley (ed.), *Medieval Industry*, Council for British Archaeology Research Report 40, Council for British Archaeology: London, 1–15.

Rahtz, P.A. 1982: Celtic Society in Somerset, AD 400–700. *Bulletin of the Board of Celtic Studies*, 30, 176–200.

Rahtz, P.A. 1985: *Convite à Arquelogica*. Basil Blackwell: Oxford and Rio de Janeiro.

Rahtz, P.A. 1988a: Archaeology and the Dead. *British Archaeological News*, 3 (4), 33.

Rahtz, P.A. 1988b: Decision-making in the Past. *Archaeological Review from Cambridge*, 7.2, 210–18.

Rahtz, P.A. and Hirst, S. 1974: *Beckery Chapel, Glastonbury, 1967–8*. Glastonbury Antiquarian Society: Glastonbury.

Rahtz, P.A. and Meeson, R.W. Forthcoming: *The Anglo-Saxon Watermill at Tamworth*. Council for British Archaeology Report. Council for British Archaeology: York.

Rahtz, P.A. and Watts, L. 1979: The End of Roman Temples in the West of Britain. In P.J. Casey (ed.), *The End of Roman Britain*, British Archaeological Reports 71, British Archaeological Reports: Oxford, 183–210.

Rahtz, P.A. and Watts, L. 1983: *Wharram Percy: The Memorial Stones of the Churchyard*. York University Archaeological Publications 1. York University Archaeological Publications: York.

Rahtz, P.A. and Watts, L. 1986: The Archaeologist on the Road to Lourdes and Santiago de Compostela. In L.A.S. Butler and R.K. Morris (eds.), *The Anglo-Saxon Church: Papers on History, Architecture and Archaeology in Honour of Dr H.M. Taylor*, Council for British Archaeological Research Reports 60, Council for British Archaeology: London, 51–73.

# Bibliography

Rahtz, P.A., Hayfield, C. and Bateman, J. 1986: *Two Roman Villas at Wharram-le-Street*. York University Archaeological Publications 2. York University Archaeological Publications: York.

Rathje, W.L. 1978: Le Projet du Garbage 1975: Historical Trade-offs. In C.L. Redman et al., *Social Archaeology Beyond Subsistence and Dating*, Academic Press: London.

Renfrew, C. 1973: *Before Civilization*. Penguin: Harmondsworth.

Robins, D. and Ross, A. 1989: *The Life and Death of a Druid Prince*. Rider: London.

Shackley, M. 1981: *Environmental Archaeology*. George Allen and Unwin: London.

Silverberg, R. 1969. *Up the Line*. Publisher not known: New York.

Twain, M. 1971 (1889): *A Connecticut Yankee at the Court of King Arthur*. Penguin: Harmondsworth.

Ucko, P. 1983a: The Politics of the Indigenous Minority. *Journal Biosocial Science Supplement*, 8, 25–40.

Ucko, P. 1983b: Australian Academic Archaeology – Aboriginal Transformations of its Aims and Practices. *Australian Archaeology*, 16, 11–26.

Ucko, P. 1988: *Academic Freedom and Apartheid*. Duckworth: London.

Von Däniken, E. 1989: *Chariots of the Gods?* Souvenir Press: London.

Vita-Finzi, C. 1969: *The Mediterranean Valleys*. Cambridge University Press: Cambridge.

Westall, R. 1976: *The Wind Eye*. Penguin: Harmondsworth.

Williamson, T. and Bellamy, L. 1983: *Ley Lines in Question*. World's Work: Tadworth.

Wilson, A. 1956: *Anglo-Saxon Attitudes*. Secker and Warburg: London.

179

# Index

# Index